hidden springs
of
HOPE

hidden springs
of
HOPE

Finding God in the Desert of Suffering

Mary Caswell Walsh

ave maria press   Notre Dame, Indiana

Mary Caswell Walsh is a psychotherapist in private practice in Chicago and Oak Park. Also a writer and spiritual director, she is the author of *The Art of Tradition: A Christian Guide to Building a Family* (Living the Good News) and *Saint Francis Celebrates Christmas* (Loyola).

All clients described in this book are composite characters drawn from the author's life experience and clinical work. Names and details have been changed to protect confidentiality.

Scripture quotations are from the *New Revised Standard Version* of the Bible, copyright © 1993 and 1989 by the Division of Christian Education of the National Council of Churches of Christ in the U.S.A. Used by permission. All rights reserved.

© 2001 by Mary C. Walsh

International Standard Book Number: 0-87793-709-5

Cover and text design by Brian C. Conley

Printed and bound in the United States of America.

Walsh, Mary Caswell.
   Hidden springs of hope : finding God in the desert of suffering / Mary
Caswell Walsh.
      p. cm.
Includes bibliographical references.
         ISBN 0-87793-709-5 (pbk.)
1. Suffering--Religious aspects--Catholic Church. 2. Prayer--
Catholic
Church. I. Title.
   BX2373.S5 W35 2001
   242'.4--dc21
                                                    00-011582

For those who have guided and supported my own healing,
especially Fr. Bernie Bush, S.J., Paul L. and Ginny T.,
Rabbi David Davis, Fr. Jim Gschwend, S.J., and
Br. Brendan Creeden, O.S.B. I am deeply grateful.

CONTENTS

Finding God in Our Suffering

The idea for this book came to me shortly after Cardinal Bernardin's illness and death. I sing in the choir at Holy Name Cathedral in Chicago and, with so many others, was deeply moved by the way in which the Cardinal embraced Christ and shared Christ in his own experience of suffering. The Cardinal discovered after his surgery that he didn't have the desire or strength to pray and told his friends, "Make sure that you pray when you're well because when you're sick, you probably won't."[1] Prayer was difficult during his illness, yet clearly God was close to him, working through him, touching others, bringing peace out of pain. As I reflected on the Cardinal's experience, I began to appreciate more fully both the difficulty and power of prayer during times of suffering.

For over twenty years I have worked as a psychotherapist, and more recently completed my internship as a chaplain. I have shared in the suffering of clients, patients, family, and friends. I have seen people blossom in the desert of their suffering; but I have seen others wither. Why is it that some blossom and not others? Why do some people turn to prayer to help with pain and others avoid prayer? Why do some people withdraw while others, like Cardinal Bernardin, reach out, radiating God's love and peace? Michael Casey, a Cistercian monk, suggests that "suffering is a door in the wall that daily routines erect around our hearts."[2] Suffering is both challenge and opportunity. When we allow suffering to open us up to God's presence, it can strengthen our souls, deepen our bonds with family and friends, and teach us what is of value and what is trivial in life. Suffering in union with God's love becomes a path to deep spiritual healing; but when we let our suffering isolate us from others or cut us off from the presence of God, suffering can diminish us, inviting us to wallow in self pity, anger, or depression. Prayer enables us to experience our suffering as a source of union and, therefore, a source of healing.

How do we pray when we don't feel like praying? How do we find a way to God when God seems distant? How can we become people who blossom rather than wither, people who open up rather than hide from the healing presence of God? I believe we can learn from those who, like Cardinal Bernardin, have found light in their experiences of darkness and peace in the midst of their pain. This book is a collection of true stories about people who have blossomed in the desert. Their stories can inspire courage and hope, offering insight into how we can welcome the Spirit of God into our suffering. Along with the stories, I include verses of scriptures which have consoled and guided men and women for centuries, and spiritual practices from a variety of religious traditions. These offer different ways of entering into prayer.

I recall a time in my own life when illness was making it difficult for me to pray. I complained of this to my spiritual director. He suggested that I quit trying so hard to pray, and start letting God do the praying in me. This may be the most helpful advice I ever received. When I began to let go of my ideas about prayer, attempting to give the Holy Spirit some freedom in my life, prayer became easier. St. Teresa of Avila writes, "It is very important for any soul that practices prayer, whether little or much, not to hold itself back and stay in one corner. Let it walk through those dwelling places which are up above, down below, and to the sides, since God has given it such great dignity. Don't force it to stay a long time in one room alone."[3]

Whether our suffering is physical, mental, spiritual, or all of the above, when we are in pain, prayer can be difficult. Prayer can become easier and more fruitful when we allow ourselves to experience God in a variety of ways: in prayers of petition and prayers of thanksgiving, in words and in silence, in scripture and in sacrament, in communion and in solitude, with the rosary and with icons. Sometimes, when we are suffering, prayer habits practiced for years are a comfort and source of strength; but sometimes suffering requires us to explore different rooms within our souls and to discover a different aspect of God's Being. These stories, words of scripture, and spiritual practices offer different rooms where the soul who is struggling may experience a new freedom and a deeper sense of God's presence.

I realize that quoting only a few verses of scripture can compromise the integrity of the text. Providing a practice from a particular spiritual tradition can give a limited and superficial experience of that tradition. One must begin somewhere, however. When we enter a new room, we cannot expect to feel as comfortable in it or know it as well as we would know a room where we have lived for many years. I have tried to mitigate this problem somewhat by providing references which offer a more in-depth approach to the given practice. I encourage readers who find a particular religious approach helpful to explore it in more depth.

Finally I have to admit my own sense of inadequacy in writing a book about suffering, prayer, and healing. I am not an expert on prayer, but I have suffered from various illnesses throughout my life and I have learned to rely on prayer as a source of grace, insight, and strength. I have been gifted by the guidance of truly holy people and blessed with healing through prayer. I have also been privileged to work, over the past twenty years, with hundreds of courageous people who have shared their struggles and victories, their suffering and their healing, their desolation and their consolation with me. I hope that their stories will be for others what they have been for me: a source of strength, hope, and inspiration, reassuring us that God's love is steadfast and accessible.

It is easy to get lost in the desert, to feel alone and become depleted, but every desert has its hidden springs. Prayer is the path to the healing waters of God's love. It is a path well marked by those who have gone before us. I pray that each of us may find our way to God. I pray that each of us may bloom in the desert of our suffering.

ONE

Sacred Space

Tom suffered from depression for many years. He knew that his mother had attempted suicide when he was a fetus, and his sister had committed suicide when she was only twenty, so his own suicidal thoughts terrified him. Sometimes the thoughts were so insistent and persistent that he could think of little else. He was not Christian, but one day, when he was having these suicidal thoughts, he noticed a church and decided to go in. The room was dark and quiet. Candles flickered at the side altars and an old woman knelt in front of a statue. Tom sat in the pew, breathing in the incense scented air. He felt safe. As long as I am sitting here, he thought, I won't hurt myself. So he sat there in the silence until the thoughts of suicide passed, and then he went home. Tom began to go to the church whenever he experienced depression and the persistent suicidal thoughts. He would sit there in the dark safety of the church until he felt strong enough to leave. Often the old women would stop on their way out and whisper, "I'm praying for you." He was grateful for their prayers.

Tom tried going to therapists, but counseling didn't seem to help. He understood his depression better, but he was still depressed. He took medication. That helped some, but not enough. He continued to have suicidal thoughts. He tried more medication and different medications without success. Oddly and inexplicably, what helped the most was sitting silently in the old church. Why? Was it the prayers of the old women? Was there some sort of power in prayer that he experienced here? Or was it the simple knowledge that he was in God's presence in the church and as long as he knew he was in God's presence he couldn't hurt himself? Was that it? But if God is present at all, Tom reasoned, he is present everywhere, not just here. Tom began to wonder how he could become aware of God's presence when he was not in the church, how he could carry the power he experienced in this sacred space with him into the world outside.

He made an appointment to see a priest and explained his situation. The priest offered to guide him as he learned to pray. He gave Tom a Bible, selected certain passages, and talked with Tom about prayer. So Tom began to pray. Every morning and every night he prayed for ten minutes, reading a few lines of scripture and mulling over them. Sometimes he would pray longer, for half an hour or even an hour. Once a week he would go back and talk with the priest about what he had read. Nothing much happened the first week or the second. It wasn't until the third week that Tom had a realization that changed his life. He realized that when he prayed nothing happened; that is, no suicidal thoughts or impulses happened. When he spent a few minutes a day in prayer, he no longer thought about killing himself. Through his sacred reading he himself became a temple of the Word. It was as if, through prayer, his body had become a sacred space in which he was finally safe.

Praying God's Word

Sacred reading, traditionally known as *lectio divina,* is a way of praying scripture developed and practiced for 1500 years in the Benedictine monastic tradition. The great Benedictine abbot John Tritheim once said that "we know Christ not by sight, not by hearing, not by touch; but we know Him by the Scriptures."[4] The Benedictine approach to reading and praying scripture involves this willingness to meet God in the Word.

In choosing a book of the Bible to read, listen to your heart. To what scripture are you drawn? St. Benedict instructed his monks to make a commitment to the book selected, reading it in its entirety. It can be helpful to consult a good commentary to give you a better understanding of the text you will be using for prayer. Having chosen a text, select a time and place free of distractions.

Michael Casey suggests that we approach the sacred text with an attitude of "reverent expectancy," beginning with a short prayer such as "Speak, Lord, for your servant is listening" (1 Sm 3:10). As most of us are used to reading quickly rather than meditatively, Casey recommends reading aloud to help one slow down, avoid distractions, and really listen.[5] Even spending ten minutes a day, or half an hour, can be deeply rewarding. We savor the text, listening for the presence of God speaking to us in the text. How much we read each day matters less than whether or not we have read in such a way as to meet God who awaits us in the Word. We begin by reading the Word (*lectio*), trying our best to understand the literal meaning. We are moved to reflect on the Word (*meditatio*), and enter into relationship with the Word, listening to how it relates personally to us and to our lives (*oratio*). As we allow God's word to resonate within us, it is no longer we who pray so much as the Spirit who prays in us, interceding for us "with sighs too deep for words" (Rom 8:26). When the Spirit invites us to rest in God's presence (*contemplatio*), we allow ourselves to be still, simply letting God love us.[6]

Reading and Prayer

Hear, O Israel: The LORD is our God, the Lord alone. You shall love the Lord your God with all your heart, and with all your soul, and with all your might. Keep these words that I am commanding you today in your heart. Recite them to your children and talk about them when you are at home and when you are away, when you lie down and when you rise (Dt 6:4-7).

How can I hear God's word
when my mind is filled with the world's noise?
Be still my mind and listen.
How can I know God's will
when my life is cluttered with my own wants?
Be still my heart and listen.

Listen that you might love the word of God.
Listen that you might live the will of God.
Listen that you might learn the way of God.
And walk with God, at peace with God, for eternity.

Be still, my soul, and listen.

Two

The Cry

She was a woman of hope, a woman of faith, and she continued to hold on to her hope that her baby would be well even after the doctors had told her that her child might have Down syndrome. When the tests were in and the doctors told her that, yes, the child did have Down syndrome, she prayed for a miracle. She would sit for hours, looking at her silent little infant, praying, hoping. The baby was so quiet, so still. What a good baby I have, she said, but her heart was troubled. She knew the child's silence wasn't normal. She called other mothers whose babies had the same condition, and she spoke to me about what she had learned, how the other babies developed, what she might expect her own child to be able to do. These women comforted her, but still she was deeply troubled. She prayed and prayed. She said to me, "We would have gone ahead and had this baby even if we'd known. He's God's creation," she said. She was being strong.

I went to see her the next day. She was smiling broadly. "You look happy," I said. "Oh yes," she said. She stroked her little son's head. "You see," she told me, "last night he cried. Such a cry!" She laughed. "I guess his lungs are just fine!" She was no longer troubled. It was the baby's cry that had reassured her. Her child needed her, and she had been able to give him the love he needed. She knew now that they would be all right.

Talking to Our Father

When Jesus taught his followers to pray, he cautioned them not to "heap up empty phrases" and reassured them that "your Father knows what you need before you ask." When we are distracted or ill or in pain, it can become impossible to think clearly or to feel reverent. Jesus reassures us that prayer is simply asking our Father for what we need. And just in case we can't even find the words to do this, God gives us words. If we have these words in our heart, we need only to repeat them over and over.

St. Ignatius of Loyola, founder of the Jesuits and author of *The Spiritual Exercises* (1533), a classic on prayer, had a conversion experience while reading the lives of the saints during a long convalescence. He suggests the following method of praying the Lord's Prayer.[7]

Begin by letting your mind repose a little. Consider where you are, where you are going, and what you desire of God. Place these needs and desires before God. Begin reciting the Our Father slowly, breathing rhythmically after each word. As you breathe, give your attention to the word. Pray as slowly and attentively as you can, but if pain or weariness makes it difficult to concentrate, don't worry. Your Father knows your needs before you ask, just as your earthly mother knew your needs before you had wit and words to speak them.

Our Father,

who art in heaven,

hallowed be thy name.

Thy kingdom come,

Thy will be done

on earth as it is in heaven.

Give us this day our daily bread

and forgive us our trespasses

as we forgive those who trespass against us.

And lead us not into temptation;

but deliver us from evil.

For thine is the kingdom and the power

and the glory

forever.

Reading and Prayer

Hear my cry, O God; listen to my prayer. From the end of the earth I call to you, when my heart is faint. . . . Let me abide in your tent forever, find refuge under the shelter of your wings (Ps 61:1-4).

Dear God, even a human parent is capable of great love and is moved to love by their child's cry of need. How can I doubt that you who are infinite love, my Creator and divine parent, will fail me when I cry to you in my human neediness? Rid me of my illusions of self-sufficiency and create in me a deep need for you. Help me to believe that you truly love me.

THREE

The Bed

She was a neat, middle-aged woman with short curly hair and a peaches and cream complexion. Petite and fair, she had been the prettiest girl in her high school class. Fifteen pounds and three children later, she was still an attractive woman, but she was no longer a happy woman. Her husband of twelve years had left her and their young children to move in with a twenty-year-old would-be model. The awful thing was, she told me, that she hadn't suspected a thing. She had believed his lies about working late. She had attributed his lack of affection to exhaustion and overwork. She had told herself that she was being selfish to expect him to spend more time with the kids or to help out around the house. After all, he was supporting them. Then one Sunday morning, he informed her, while eating the bacon and eggs she had cooked for him, that he didn't love her anymore. He was tired of her. He loved someone else. And he was leaving. Then he had packed his bags and left. She had begged him to come back, to see a counselor, to work things out. But he had refused. It was over and he was gone.

That night she had gone into their bedroom, but she couldn't bear to lie down on the bed they had shared. She curled up on the couch with a blanket. She didn't sleep. All night long she thought about what she should have said and what she could have done. She thought about throwing his breakfast eggs onto the white shirt she had washed and ironed the night before. She thought about the names she could have called him. She came up with a hundred scathing rejoinders and sophisticated comebacks, and then recalled numbly her actual response: a shocked and helpless silence. What would she tell the children?

Night after night she slept on the couch, quietly crying herself to sleep. Their marriage bed became a place to fold laundry and sort mail. Unable to overcome her sense of rejection, she decided to get counseling. She was an intelligent, attractive, and highly competent woman, but she felt like a failure and a dowd. In the weeks that followed, as she worked through her painful feelings of betrayal and loss, her inability to sleep in their bed became a symbol for her of her need to cling to her faithless husband, and of her fear of living without him. She would know she was beginning to heal, she decided, when their bed became her bed and she was able to sleep there again.

She was a woman of prayer, and each day she would pray for the courage to go on. She set tasks for herself, inching toward her goal of sleeping in the bed. The first week she folded the laundry piled up on the bed and put it away. The next week she sorted the piles of papers and put them away. The week after that she stripped the bed, washed the sheets, and made it up fresh. Finally, the day came when she was ready to turn back the covers and get into bed. She knelt on the carpet at the foot of the bed, praying for the inner strength to face life as a single mom, praying for the peace to accept her loss. Then she got into bed, pulled the covers up to her chin, and tried to sleep.

The next morning she was awakened by a brilliant light shining through the window. The light was warm on her face. It filled her with a deep peace and a new strength. She had done it. She had slept soundly in her own bed. She had had a good night and she was going to have a good day. What a beautiful sunny day it was. She got out of the bed and began to make it. Straightening the sheets, she said to herself: "I'm going to be all right and my children will be all right." As she fluffed the pillows she looked out the window. It was then that she realized that the blinds were still shut and the heavy drapes closed.

Listening to Our Bodies

The body is often seen as an enemy to prayer because our appetites can be such a distraction and our bodily weaknesses, aches, and pains can make it difficult to think about anything or anyone else. Yet scripture calls our body the temple of the spirit. This does not cease to be true when we are suffering. Instead of fighting with our body, sometimes it is important to listen to it, to its needs and wants and desires.

The following prayer evolved out of a relaxation exercise one man used to help cope with the anxiety he felt about having surgery. It may help us relax, but it is most beneficial in helping us pay loving attention to our bodies, placing the needs of our bodies before our Creator.

Choose a comfortable position; lying down is preferable. Breathe deeply and slowly for a few moments, allowing your mind to become still and your body relaxed. Continue to breathe slowly as you focus on your feet, first one and then the other. Be aware of your feet. How do they feel? Relaxed, tired? Is there any pain? Take your time. As you focus on your feet, simply be aware of any feelings or thoughts that emerge. If a need emerges, put this need before God. If there is pain, you might ask for healing; if weakness, you might ask for strength. Or perhaps you will pray for the peace to accept pain and weakness. Perhaps you will become aware of how much you depend on your feet and how little you think about them. Then you might wish to thank God for them. Perhaps no thoughts or feelings will emerge. Be aware of the silence for a moment, then move on to your ankles and pay attention to your ankles as you did to your feet, being aware of feelings and needs and lifting these up to the Creator. When you are ready, move on to your calves, your knees, and so on up your body. You do not need to take a lot of time. The point is to be still and aware of your body, respecting its needs, listening to its feelings, being grateful for its service. Pay loving attention to each part of your body. When you are finished, be still for a moment, then thank God for your body. Invite the Spirit of God to come and make its home within your body.

Reading and Prayer

Blessed be the God and Father of our Lord Jesus Christ, the Father of mercies and the God of all consolation, who consoles us in all our affliction, so that we may be able to console those who are in any affliction with the consolation with which we ourselves are consoled by God. For just as the sufferings of Christ are abundant for us, so also our consolation is abundant through Christ (2 Cor 1:3-5).

Dear God, I have been rejected by those I loved most dearly. I have been misunderstood, mistreated, and hurt deeply. I try to go on as if nothing has happened; I make-believe I don't care and don't need anyone. But you see me, Lover of my soul. You see me in the middle of the night when I cannot sleep. I am afraid if I start crying, I'll never stop. I'm afraid if I let you love me, you too will criticize me, ridicule me, reject me. Or worse, ignore me. You were rejected and scorned, even put to death. Each day you are given up to suffering and death, for our suffering is your suffering. As a child's pain is pain to his parent, as a beloved's pain is pain to her lover, so you have made our suffering your suffering. As I share in your suffering, may I share also in the comfort only you can give. And may I become a source of comfort to others.

FOUR

Lion's Dance

My first visit to Chicago, the city in which I now live, was the summer of the 1968 Democratic Convention. It was a very hot summer, in more ways than one. I had driven cross country to visit my brother and his wife who lived in a small apartment on the south side. Dwight was a doctoral student in theology at the University of Chicago and had a coffee house ministry, working with the Blackstone Rangers. I was a dancer back then and got a job teaching dancing at a parochial school. I quickly realized that as a young white girl from the country my experiences were quite different from my street smart black city-kid students.

I had been teaching for only a couple of weeks when I met and struck up a friendship with a tall, muscular, good looking African American who had been nicknamed Hercules by his friends. He was an accomplished wrestler and African dancer, and our friendship began by exchanging dance steps. He offered to teach African dancing to my students. I obtained permission from the nuns, and Hercules arrived dressed in a loin cloth and spear. This got the kids' attention. I was concerned that the nuns might not approve, but they, taking in his intelligent and gracious manner and the obvious adoration in the eyes of their students, let us have our dance class. Hercules elicited the help of the students to clear a large open space in the gym, pushing metal school desks and chairs to the side. He gathered the children together at one end of the room and coached them in being villagers for the dance. He selected two children to play his drums, teaching them rhythms and encouraging the villagers to clap and shout. One of the smallest boys, a child who was routinely teased by the other children because of his size and homeliness, stood apart in his customary isolation. He was a sad, lonely, awkward child who somehow inspired ridicule. I had tried often and unsuccessfully to draw him out. It was this boy whom Hercules chose to be the lion. Taking his spear, the six foot lion hunter began dancing as the villagers clapped and the drummers drummed and, to my surprise, the sad little boy lion began to run. The hunter chased the lion, dancing and leaping with great energy and beautiful movement. In a wide circle they ran, hunter and hunted, as the villagers cheered the hunter, chanting, "Hunter! Hunter!" When the little lion was at last caught by the hunter, the villagers roared their approval.

Then the hunter gave his spear to the boy. Crouching and snarling the six foot hunter transformed himself into a great muscular lion. The little boy took the spear and standing tall began to dance. By now everyone was into it. The little hunter danced with unexpected agility, but the villagers did not cheer him. Instead they now cheered the impressive lion as he leapt and danced around the room with the small hunter leaping after him. Faster and faster the lion ran with the hunter in close pursuit, the drums beating louder and louder, and the villagers crying, "Lion! Lion!" The little lion hunter ignored the crowd, intent on the hunt, his heart in the dance. A desk stood in the lion's path and the lion leaped over it. The villagers gasped and applauded. The little hunter, close on his heels, with the desk in his path, leapt into the air. We held our breath. In a single graceful bound the little boy sailed over the desk, clearing it and landing squarely on the gym floor. A huge cheer went up and the villagers began to chant, "Hunter! Hunter!" The little hunter's T-shirt was wet with sweat. Absorbed in the dance, he didn't seem to notice the cries of the crowd. Waving the spear in the air, the little hunter closed in for the kill. He lunged forward and then it was over. The great lion lay on the gym floor, felled by the brave hunter. And then, in a moment of startling tenderness, the little hunter knelt and hunter and lion embraced.

Kids and teachers shouted with enthusiasm, encircling the boy. They hoisted him onto their shoulders and paraded him victoriously around the room. The boy laughed and waved his arms in the air. The child who had been the object of ridicule in a moment of self-forgetting had claimed his glory. Hunter and hunted had embraced.

Learning From Creation

Human beings often act with an arrogant disregard for the rest of creation. Most spiritual traditions challenge us to seek human healing by learning to live in greater harmony with creation. The hunter must respect the animal whose body sustains him. The gatherer must bless the plants that nourish her. Too often we are motivated not by a human need for sustenance but by our drive to dominate. Our thirst for power poisons the very waters which slake our thirst. Saint Francis of Assisi insisted that obedience to the Holy Spirit "subjects a man to everyone on earth, and not only to men, but to all the beasts as well and to the wild animals."[8]

To experience a greater harmony with creation, try reflecting on the nature of a certain creature or plant. Choose a living thing for which you feel some affinity, attraction, curiosity, or admiration. Observe this living creature, reflecting on its behavior, its beauty, its place in creation. Approach it humbly, as one seeking to hear in it that word spoken by the Creator which only this creature can speak. How does God care for it? How does it respond to God's care? What does this say to you about your relationship with your Creator?

Reading and Prayer

The wolf shall live with the lamb, the leopard shall lie down with the kid, the calf and the lion and the fatling together, and a little child shall lead them. The cow and the bear shall graze, their young shall lie down together; and the lion shall eat straw like the ox. The nursing child shall play over the hole of the asp, and the weaned child shall put its hand on the adder's den. They will not hurt or destroy on all my holy mountain; for the earth will be full of the knowledge of the LORD as the waters cover the sea (Is 11:6-9).

Dear God, as I ponder the beauty and goodness of your creation, I am filled with wonder. How beautiful is the hawk, circling the tops of the pine trees. There is such grace in its flight. I long to be like the hawk, at ease with power. I long to be simply myself in your presence.

Divine Beauty, help me to surrender to your power. Help me to live a life of grace and goodness. Let me not be discouraged by those who treat me as less than I am. Nor let me be tempted to pretend I am better than I am. Help me to be no more and no less than all you have created me to be, that my being may reflect your glory.

How beautiful is the hawk, so simply itself in your presence, so at ease with your power. I long to be like the hawk.

FIVE

The Song

I met Mary when I was working at the hospital. She had suffered a stroke which had resulted in loss of speech and impairment of her muscular coordination. No one knew how much her mind had been damaged or how much she understood. Time would tell. She lay in the hospital bed with her white hair waving about her pale face. Her sister often sat in a chair at her side, chatting comfortably. It was clear that they were very close. Most of the time Mary appeared cheerful. She made eye contact when you spoke to her and often tried to talk, making repetitive incomprehensible sounds. It was when she tried to talk that she grew frustrated. Her sister and I tried to include her in our conversations, guessing from her expression what her reaction was; but her lack of words was isolating. Her sister worried and fretted on the days when Mary was restless and uncomfortable. Other days she would tell me stories about their life together before Mary's stroke. They were good people, kind people, who had shared a sisterly affection that most would envy. The days and weeks passed with only minor improvements in Mary's condition. She regained some movement in her hand but was still unable to speak. She grew more and more frustrated by this.

On the Feast of the Assumption I came to visit Mary and her sister.

"It's your feast day," I smiled at Mary, "so we should do something special." Usually we prayed together, but this day I decided to sing a song in honor of Mary. Softly, I began to sing "Salve Regina." Mary's sister joined in, taking Mary's hand in hers. And then, to our amazement, Mary began to sing. She sang the words of the long loved hymn in a sweet, gentle voice, each word clear and perfect. Tears welled up in her eyes and ran down her face. Her sister began to cry, and so did I. Mary and her sister continued to sing the song over and over as I ran to get the speech therapist. They went on to other Marian hymns I'd never learned, and these were followed by "Take Me Out to the Ball Game," "Tea for Two," and "Oh Susannah." It was as if they were afraid to stop singing, clinging to the magic of the moment. Mary was giddy with happiness.

The therapist explained that the part of the brain that handles singing is different from the part of the brain that handles speech, so sometimes a person who can't speak words is able to sing them. Mary could not speak, but she could sing. The discovery that she could sing lifted from her the burden of isolation, fed her sense of hope, and gave her a bridge to traverse on her way back to health and wholeness. In time, Mary regained her speech and much of her mobility. She was released from the hospital and went home with her sister. I have not seen them since, but I cannot sing "Salve Regina" without thinking of them.

Seeing With an Icon

Often when we are ill or suffering, we find ourselves surrounded by ugliness. Ugly hospital gowns. Drab hospital furniture, antiseptic smells, and minty green walls. Even if we are at home, we may not have the energy to keep up with the housework or go for a walk in beautiful surroundings. And yet, beauty is a great spiritual resource for most people. As a therapist, when I ask clients what their primary source for inner peace, strength, and joy is, the majority of them name beauty. Just as singing opened Mary up in a way that speech could not, prayers which inspire an awareness of beauty open us up to God in profoundly healing ways. Because beauty can touch people of all ages, the weak and strong, healthy and ill, it is both powerful and universal. St. Augustine, longing for the beauty of God, writes in his *Confession*, "Too late have I loved you, Beauty so old and so new" (X, 27).

One approach to prayer which awakens our sense of beauty is prayer with icons. Icons are not pretty pictures, they are windows opening onto Divine Beauty. St. John Damascene writes, "The beauty of the images moves me to contemplation, as a meadow delights the eyes and subtly infuses the soul with the glory of God."[9]

Choose an icon which attracts or interests you. Icons can be obtained at religious goods stores or by mail.[10] To pray with the icon, spend a few moments becoming still. Let your eyes take in the picture, silently opening your heart to receive whatever the Spirit wishes to give. St. Nicholas De Cusa, the fifteenth-century mystic, reminds us that "only because God first looks at him, can man desire to look at God."[11] Let the beauty of the icon draw your heart and mind into union with God, who is Divine Beauty. Do not expect the icon to appeal to you immediately. Henri Nouwen suggests, "It is only gradually, after a patient, prayerful presence that they start speaking to us. And as they speak, they speak more to our inner than to our outer senses. They speak to the heart that searches for God."[12]

Reading and Prayer

Listen to me, you that pursue righteousness, you that seek the LORD. Look to the rock from which you were hewn, and to the quarry from which you were dug. Look to Abraham your father and to Sarah who bore you; for he was but one when I called him, but I blessed him and made him many. For the LORD will comfort Zion; he will comfort all her waste places, and will make her wilderness like Eden, her desert like the garden of the LORD; joy and gladness will be found in her, thanksgiving and the voice of song (Is 51:1-3).

Dear God, how beautiful is your creation, how beautiful your works. Your beauty is manifest in the art and music of your children. Your beauty comforts me, refreshes me, and turns my deserts into gardens. And yet, how often I am blind to your beauty. I do not notice the sunrise as I hurry to get ready for work or the flower bravely poking its blossomed face through the crack in the sidewalk. I don't notice the bright, curious eyes of the child in front of me in the supermarket line or the way the silver hair of the old woman on the bus catches the light. The world you have created is not always comfortable. It is not always comprehensible. But it is always indescribably and unquestionably beautiful. How often I think you are a hidden God. And yet, not a day goes by, not even an hour, no, not even a minute, in which you do not reveal yourself to me through beauty. If only I would open my soul eyes and see your glory revealed, creation transfigured, God manifest and dwelling among us.

Six

The Obsession

Jim came to me for counseling because his obsession with Internet pornography was causing problems in his marriage. As we discussed his problem, Jim revealed that he had had persistent temptations to sadomasochistic thoughts since adolescence. He had grown up watching his parents' violent fights and, often enough, had experienced the brunt of their anger directed at him in verbal assaults and ridicule. His feelings, both toward his parents and himself, were a troubling mixture of love and hatred. He was terrified of his anger, plagued with guilt, hated violence, and yet, to his disgust, was sexually aroused by it. He couldn't imagine sharing this with his spouse. Therapy provided an outlet for his frustration, reassurance that he was, in spite of these thoughts, a decent person, and insight into why he had these thoughts; but he continued to have them. We looked for ways of substituting other thoughts for these troubling ones, but this was slow going. In the end, Jim's breakthrough came not from therapy but from prayer.

Jim was a devout man and took prayer seriously. He discovered, however, that the more he gave himself to prayer, the more deeply he was troubled by these thoughts. For a while he even gave up on prayer; but not for long. One day it occurred to him that rather than trying to keep these thoughts away from his prayer, he would bring his prayer to them. Rather than struggle against these thoughts, he decided to invite Christ into them.

It took him two weeks to work up the nerve. These thoughts were dark and hidden. Somehow he could be open with them on the Internet where he was anonymous, but feared placing the thoughts before God, even in the privacy of his heart. Before God, he was not anonymous. Jim prayed for the grace to open his heart fully to God.

When he was finally able to, Jim simply invited Christ into his ugly, obsessive fantasy. In his imagination, he saw Christ looking on silently and then Christ spoke softly saying, "Jim, you don't have to do this anymore." With that, the thoughts left, dissolving into a peaceful silence.

Jim enjoyed peace of mind after this for many months. Eventually, unexpectedly, the thoughts did return, but now Jim knew that he had only to invite Christ into the deepest recesses of his heart and mind to be restored to peace once again.

Thinking Holy Thoughts

The fourth- and fifth-century desert fathers and mothers were the first, and are still among the best, cognitive therapists in history. Living in the deserts of Egypt, Syria, and Palestine, they left behind worldly ties and possessions, seeking in the emptiness and freedom of the desert greater purity of heart and intimacy with the Divine. They discovered, however, that although they had left their possessions behind, they had brought their minds along. To achieve their goal of more perfect love of God, they needed to renounce not only their possessions but their possessive thoughts as well.

Anyone who has tried to let go of an old, unhealthy, and limiting way of life will have encountered the same problem. The alcoholic who quits drinking finds himself fantasizing about martinis. The overeater who has lost forty pounds can't get the thought of chocolate out of her head. The adulterer no sooner decides to be faithful, than he begins fantasizing about another woman. Whatever we gave up for Lent is bound to occupy our thoughts until Easter.

When we are active in the world, we are often unconscious of our thoughts. We tune them out, easily distracted by the noise and demands of our lives. However, if God has brought us, through suffering, into the desert, we may begin to hear these thoughts, just as the desert monks did. We may long to still our inner noise and know the peace of God's silence in our hearts, but not know how. If this is the case, the teachings of the desert monks may be helpful. These teachings are profound and extensive. I cannot even begin to do them justice, but I encourage those who are troubled by distracting and unsettling thoughts to consult John Cassian's *Conferences*, or, for those looking for a contemporary and accessible introduction to these teachings, Mary Margaret Funk's *Thoughts Matter*.

For our purposes, I wish to share two very simple, albeit difficult, suggestions which come to us from these teachings. These insights, as I have already noted, provide the backbone of much work in cognitive therapy. First, we must notice our thoughts, no matter how uncomfortable they make us. We need to pay special attention to those thoughts which are most troubling and persistent. Journaling or sharing with a wise and discreet friend can help us gain awareness of these thoughts. Rather than resisting the thoughts, we shine a light on them.

Second, we either rethink the thought or place a prayer alongside the thought. To rethink the thought, first we name the recurring thought (for example, wanting a cigarette, or rehashing an old resentment). Next we choose a substitute thought (for example, I want to be free of addiction, or I want to forgive so and so). Some people find it helpful to write the substitute thought down on a three by five card and simply pull out and read the card when needed. To place a prayer alongside the thought, we can choose a prayer from scripture or our own prayer, and whenever the thought occurs, we recite the prayer. The prayer from Psalm 70 discussed in Chapter Fifteen is recommended by John Cassian: "O God, come to my assistance, O Lord, make haste to help me." Or we could choose a single meaningful word, such as "love" or "peace" or "faith" that contains within it both our desire for God and our need for freedom from whatever enslaves and distracts us. Whenever the troublesome thought occurs, we consciously choose to think these holy thoughts.

To confront the ugly, poisonous thoughts that infest our minds takes courage. I know of few things more difficult than rethinking these thoughts, or bringing them into the light of prayer; but I also know of no other spiritual exercise more efficacious to our mental and spiritual health.

Cassian reassures us that "where a man is anxious to cleanse his heart, and has steeled his heart's purpose against the attack of any one fault, it is impossible for him not to have a general dread of all other faults as well, and take similar care of them" (*Conferences*, V, xiv). Our efforts in this can have far-reaching effects. But Cassian also warns us not to take credit for our victories. He reminds us that we cannot possibly gain victory in this struggle by our own strength and efforts. Therefore, when God grants us victory, we give thanks, singing with the psalmist, "Blessed be the LORD, for he has wondrously shown his steadfast love to me when I was beset as a city under siege. . . . Love the LORD, all you his saints. The LORD preserves the faithful . . ." (Ps 31:21, 23).

Reading and Prayer

You desire truth in the inward being; therefore teach me wisdom in my secret heart. Purge me with hyssop, and I shall be clean; wash me, and I shall be whiter than snow. Let me hear joy and gladness; let the bones that you have crushed rejoice. Hide your face from my sins, and blot out all my iniquities. Create in me a clean heart, O God, and put a new and right spirit within me. Do not cast me away from your presence, and do not take your holy spirit from me. Restore to me the joy of your salvation, and sustain in me a willing spirit (Ps 51:6-12).

———————— 🌿 ————————

God, our Father,
Lead me out of slavery to self
as once you led your people
out of their slavery in Egypt.

Jesus, our Redeemer,
Help me to turn away
from vain and empty thoughts
as Mary turned away from the empty tomb,
that, like her, I might experience your resurrection.

Holy Spirit, our Comforter,
Intercede for me, obtaining for me the grace
to live with such purity of heart
and holiness of thought
that I might never cause you sadness.
May you, my Divine Guest,
live joyfully within my soul.

———————— 🌿 ————————

SEVEN

Touch

In the last year of her drinking and drug use, Miriam had imagined herself to be a living corpse. Her hands were numb. Stocking glove neuropathy, the doctor called it; but to her it was the outward sign of an inward dying she had felt helpless to prevent. When she had been drinking, she didn't want to feel. The feelings were unbearable and made her long to die. She feared the feelings, but now she also feared this numbness. She had tried AA, not because she thought it would really help. She didn't really believe anyone could help her. But she had run out of places to go and run out of people willing to listen. She couldn't stand being alone with herself.

These people were strangers and yet they seemed to understand her innermost thoughts. They poured her coffee when her hands shook too badly to manage, without making her feel embarrassed. She drank coffee and smoked and ate cookies and listened. And something happened. What had happened? She had one hour sober and then another and then a day and a night and a day. She was too sick and too tired to question it. She just did as she was told. They told her, "Ask

God for your sobriety in the morning, don't take the first drink or drug, and say thanks at night." Simple. She could do that, couldn't she? She asked for her sobriety in the mornings when she washed her hands, so she wouldn't forget. She vaguely remembered a prayer her grandmother had taught her, something about asking God to help you return to him as clean and pure as you had been when first created. Had she ever felt clean and pure? That innocence seemed so far away now, irretrievable; but she did as she was told.

Every morning she washed her hands and prayed for her sobriety, and she went to the meetings and drank coffee and listened, and at night she got on her knees and said thank-you. But the water on her hands did not feel like water; her hands were too numb to feel. And when people asked her how she felt, she didn't know what to say. She didn't know what she felt anymore. She was like a corpse. Dead inside. Empty and dead. But she stayed sober, one day at a time.

Then one morning, she awoke, climbed out of bed, and went to the bathroom. She turned on the faucet and began to wash her hands, saying her morning prayer, "Dear God, keep me sober this day . . . ," and she could feel it. Cool and wet. She could feel the water on her hands. She was no longer a living corpse. She was alive. She felt more, far more, than the water on her hands. The feeling welled up inside her like a great river. Her eyes filled with tears. "Thank you, thank you, thank you." The tears ran down her cheeks. She cupped her hands under the faucet until they filled with water, then bathed her face. "Thank you, thank you, thank you." The water ran down her face and neck. "Thank you for my feelings. Thank you for my life." Her heart overflowed with gratitude, a deep and cleansing gratitude for life.

Washing in Healing Waters

Ritual bathing, an ancient spiritual practice, is an act of purification, renewal, and rebirth. It is an ancient Jewish ritual to pray as you wash your hands in the morning. Why in the morning? The rabbis teach that in the morning "we are like a new creation." Rabbi Shlomo of Karlin suggests: "You should think that in this water also there is the life-power of God, blessed be He, and if it were not there the water would pass out of existence. Think of this water as linked to its spiritual root, which is the spiritual water, the pure water that purifies; and that is what this water signifies."[13]

The Jewish traditions of ritual bathing are the root of Christian baptism. Christians using this practice may want to recall their baptism, renewing their baptismal vows by praying simply: "I reaffirm my faith in God, the Father, the Son, and the Holy Spirit. Amen."

Begin by pouring water over your hands three times. Cup your fingers with your hands touching and reaching out. As you make this gesture of openness to God, be aware of your need and desire to be cleansed, healed, and purified by the Divine Presence.[14]

Next, wash your face, recalling that you are made in the Divine Image.[15] As you cleanse your mouth, pray that the words of your mouth, the meditations of your heart, and the work of your hands may be pleasing to your Creator.

Reading and Prayer

A new heart I will give you, and a new spirit I will put within you; and I will remove from your body the heart of stone and give you a heart of flesh (Ez 36:26).

Dear God, sometimes I am afraid to feel too much and too deeply. I am afraid I will be overwhelmed. I am afraid to love too much, and so I hold back. I am afraid to care too much, so I become cynical and pretend I don't care at all. I am afraid to hope too much, for fear I will be disappointed and disillusioned. I shut off my feelings, sometimes with alcohol or drugs, sometimes with just keeping too busy to feel, sometimes by distracting myself in a thousand different ways. Heal me of this fear, for it is killing me. I do not want to die. I want to live. And to be alive is to feel. Teach me to be grateful for my feelings.

I thank you for the pain which reminds me of my need for you. I thank you for the peace that reassures me of your presence. I thank you for the joy I feel when I am in love and for the sorrow that calls me to seek an everlasting love. I thank you for the anger that springs from my thirst for justice and for the guilt that calls me to repentance. I thank you for hope that gives me the energy to go on and for the weariness that tells me it is time to rest. I thank you for the loneliness that calls me out of my selfishness and into the company of others and for the desire for solitude which calls me to spend time alone with you. I thank you for my feelings, dear God. I thank you for my life.

EIGHT

Mona

I first met Mona when I was sixteen and working at a program for the children of farm workers in a run-down area of San Jose, colloquially called Sal se Puedo (meaning, "get out if you can"). She was the youngest of her family's eleven children and lived in extreme poverty. Each Saturday while the parents studied English, I watched the children, playing with them and teaching them a little English in the process. Most of the children played happily together, but Mona sat off by herself. Did she like to be alone? Was her English not as good as the others? Did she feel embarrassed? Was she depressed? Looking back with the eyes of a therapist, I wonder if Mona needed psychological help; but at the time we just assumed she was frightened and withdrawn. Mona at five was a full-grown stone. I talked to her: no response. I brought her little gifts: no expression. Sometimes we shared crackers and juice. Sometimes I told her stories. I brought various games to play with her. Sometimes I spoke to her in Spanish and at other times in English, but mostly we said noth-ing. I came to feel close to Mona, and yet she never spoke and never even smiled. She watched me with her large dark eyes in silence. After awhile her silence no longer unnerved me. I no longer needed to fill up the silence with stories and jokes. As I became more comfortable with Mona, Mona seemed to become more comfortable with me. Sometimes we walked together. Sometimes we sat together, doing nothing, saying nothing. I began to look forward to the silent moments I spent each week with Mona.

When the last Saturday came, I had no expectations. The project would end in a drizzle of unfinished business, paperwork, evaluations, and with them, my last chance to be with Mona.

We would sit silently, perhaps watching some pudgy pigeon or a butterfly. I would give her the daffodil I had brought with me, and she would take it without looking up, without saying a word, and I would leave Sal se Puedo and Mona and the silent Saturdays behind me. I couldn't help feeling a little disappointed. Mona had allowed me to enter her prison. At least it seemed a prison to me, a world shut off from others. She had shared her silence with me, but she remained within. I wanted to leave a window, even a crack in her walls, but I instinctively knew I had to respect her walls. For some reason known only to her, she needed them.

That Saturday seemed the same as every other Saturday. We sat in the long silence. Mona stirred the dirt with a stick. I stared at the clouds slowly moving across the sky. When it was time to leave I went to get the daffodil I had brought for Mona, still fresh in the Dixie cup of water in the coat room. My farewell.

She held the daffodil, looking up at me with those still dark eyes. And then, for the first time in three months, Mona smiled. Sometimes we see cracks in prisons we thought impenetrable. Sometimes we leave daffodils behind. Sometimes endings are beginnings. Sometimes.

Discovering Silence

Interior noise is one of the great difficulties many of us face when we go to pray. We live in a noisy world, and the noise seeps into our hearts and minds. We carry this noise with us into prayer. We worry about what we ought to be doing, fantasize about what we would like to have, fret about what we're not getting done. Jingles from inane commercials and the whine of the air conditioner claim our attention. Any sort of mental anguish tends to increase the volume of our inner noise. Isidore said:

> Prayer is a work of the heart, not of the lips, for God does not pay attention to the words of the one who is praying to him, but rather to his or her heart. It is better to pray in the silence of the heart than to pray only with words, without the mind paying attention. [16]

Prayer is about listening, but it is difficult to listen in a noisy room. How, then, do we silence this interior babble?

I don't think interior silence is something we do. I think interior silence is something God does within us. Our job is to prepare to receive this gift. There are many techniques of prayer which can help us become centered and focused while we are praying. These can be helpful, but it can also be helpful to pay attention not only to our designated times of prayer but to the whole of our noisy, busy lives. If we live with more silence in our daily lives, we may find it easier to receive God's gift of silence during our time of prayer.

I have a friend who gave up unnecessary conversations for Lent one year. No, she didn't stop talking, she just tried to avoid unnecessary talking. Of course, to decide whether or not a conversation was necessary, she first had to stop and think about what she was going to say. She quickly realized how often she spoke without thinking. As she focused on talking less, she found that she began to listen more. She had always prided herself on being a good listener, but she discovered that she was not as good a listener as she'd thought. Sometimes she interrupted people or became inattentive when others were talking. At first, as she tried to abide by her Lenten discipline, she felt irritated. She didn't like facing her own imperfection, and she found it difficult to exercise discipline over her eager tongue. As she got the hang of it, however, she started to enjoy the exercise. She began to feel more peace and energy than she had felt in years. And her prayer life grew deeper, more satisfying and fruitful.

If you have a lot of interior noise, consider trying an exercise that will bring a little extra silence into your everyday life. Like my friend, you might try to talk less and listen more attentively to what others have to say. Or you might try driving without the radio on or turning off the TV in the evenings. Notice the sources of unnecessary noise in your life and make a commitment to choose silence. I believe that interior silence is a gift from God. We must, however, ready ourselves to receive God's gifts.

Reading and Prayer

Listen, you that are deaf; and you that are blind, look up and see! Who is blind but my servant, or deaf like my messenger whom I send? Who is blind like my dedicated one, or blind like the servant of the LORD? He sees many things, but does not observe them; his ears are open, but he does not hear. . . . Who among you will give heed to this, who will attend and listen for the time to come? (Is 42:18-20, 23).

Dear God, deafened by the noise of our world
and the cacophony of our lives, we have such trouble hearing
anything, anyone. Is this why you come to us as a single
Word?

Nine

Legion

I was asked to speak to Joe by the nurses on the unit. Joe was causing problems and the nurses were fed up. Joe was a very angry man. He began by complaining about the nurses. Then he complained about his doctor. Then he started in on his family. I had been listening patiently, thinking he needed to vent, but I was beginning to realize that he wasn't winding down. At this point I didn't think my visit was serving much constructive purpose other than to distract Joe from his call bell. That was probably the nurse's intent. I was trying to think of a graceful way to exit when I began to realize that all the family members Joe was so angry at had the same name. They were all named John. I looked down at his chart. John Joseph. "You're name's John," I said. "I don't like John," he replied. "John's an asshole." "Which John is an asshole?" I asked. "They all are," he said. He explained that he had six brothers and they were all named John and they were all assholes. I excused myself and went to the nurses station. I asked the nurse about Joe's family and learned that he had one long-suffering sister named Mabel. No brothers. Did he have an illness that made him delusional? No, not that they knew of. How about meds that might make him think he was six or seven people at once? The nurse gave me an odd look. No. I suggested they get a psychiatric evaluation and went back in to talk to John Joseph.

There was a worn-out Bible on his bedside table. I asked what scripture he liked. He began talking animatedly about a passage from the Letter of James in which the sick are anointed.

That afternoon Joe was evaluated by a psychiatrist and diagnosed as delusional. I visited him not long after the doctor's visit. He immediately began telling me about his brothers and how angry he was with them. He said he was angry with them because they were sick. He told me they needed to be anointed. I checked the chart again. Joe was Catholic. His condition was terminal. "Do you want to be anointed?" I asked. No, he didn't want to be anointed. He wasn't sick. He wanted his brothers to be anointed. It was his brothers who were sick. I explained that I was a chaplain intern, not a priest, but I would try to get someone to come.

I wasn't at the hospital when the priest came. The nurses told me that he had arrived that evening and spent a long time with Joe. That didn't surprise me. "He's been real quiet this morning," the nurse told me, with obvious relief. When I went in Joe was lying on his bed, staring out the window. "I called my brothers," he told me. His voice was no longer angry, but quiet. Then at length he told me how he had called each of his brothers named John and how he had forgiven each of them. That afternoon, Joe was transferred to a psychiatric unit.

I believe that somehow through that anointing God penetrated the labyrinthine maze of Joe's mind with the healing light of love. And if God can get through to Joe, I tell myself, God can get through to me too.

Praying When We're Angry

When we are suffering we are likely to feel anger. Sometimes we are angry with the people we love. Sometimes we are angry with ourselves. Sometimes our anger is directed at God. How can God stand by and let me suffer like this? I thought God loved me! Many people feel that it is irreverent to feel angry with God. Instead of expressing their anger and dealing with it, they simply give God the cold shoulder, and quit praying. Or they bury their true feelings inside and approach God with a polite but closed heart.

Scripture is filled with stories of holy people who experienced anger. Moses became angry with his flock on more than one occasion. David grew angry with God when Uzzah was killed. Psalmists and prophets express their anger and frustration in vivid language. The moneychangers at the temple experienced Jesus' anger, and scripture often describes God as angry with his people. I think we have to assume, given scripture, that anger is not antithetical to holiness. But what do we do with this anger? Do we allow it to turn us against God? Do we let it make us vindictive, resentful, or destructive? One Jewish practice suggests that we turn to God with our anger, complaining to God.

Begin by telling God just how you feel. Tell God why you are so angry. Tell God you want to be free of this anger, and "nag" God until, with God's help, you are rid of it. It's not that God needs to be nagged, but sometimes we need to experience our own commitment to change. It is also a Jewish practice to touch a holy object when angry, such as the fringe of one's prayer shawl or the Torah. A Christian might touch the Bible or a medal. The idea is to shift our attention onto God. Once we remember God and turn to God, opening our hearts in all honesty, our emotions are likely to regain their balance and the anger will begin to dissipate.[17]

Reading and Prayer

Are any among you suffering? They should pray. Are any cheerful? They should sing songs of praise. Are any among you sick? They should call for the elders of the church and have them pray over them, anointing them with oil in the name of the Lord. The prayer of faith will save the sick, and the Lord will raise them up; and anyone who has committed sins will be forgiven. Therefore confess your sins to one another, and pray for one another, so that you may be healed. The prayer of the righteous is powerful and effective (Jas 5:13-16).

Heal me, Divine Physician. I do the things I hate. I think thoughts I don't want to think, and I desire things I know aren't good for me. Heal not only my sickness but cleanse me of the fears, passions, anger, and self-destructiveness which continue to sicken my soul. Anoint me with the healing balm of your forgiveness and love. Heal my inner divisions and make me whole. Heal my relationships and help me to live in unity and communion with family, friends, and even my enemies. Heal me, Divine Physician.

TEN

Neshama, Breath of God

Her white hair lay in wisps on her forehead; her thin face with the finely chiseled nose and high cheekbones had a quiet elegance. Even in a hospital gown with oxygen tubes coming out her nose, she was every inch a lady. She spoke in a whisper, barely audible over the background bustle of the hospital. "I can't breathe," she said, struggling for air. Her kidneys were failing, the doctor had said, and it was only a matter of time. She wanted company, but it was difficult to speak, so we sat awhile in silence, her frail white hand in mine.

"*Neshama*," I told her, "is one of the oldest words for soul in the Hebrew scriptures. It means *breath*." We prayed together, breathing together, imagining that with every breath we were breathing in God. I felt a deep peace, sitting there, breathing with her. Her eyes lit up when her daughter, a bright-eyed woman, came. She was so proud of her daughter and clearly they were very close. The daughter regaled her mother and me with wonderful memories of their life together—lively stories that made her mother chuckle and grin.

I was not there when she died, but her daughter called and told me about it. Her breathing continued to be labored. She closed her eyes and slept. Her daughter, knowing the end was near, took off her shoes and climbed into the hospital bed with her mother. She lay there watching her mother breathing. "Someone told me," her daughter said, "that being with her when she died would be a spiritual experience, so as I watched her breathing, I waited for her last breath, and wondered if I would have some sort of spiritual experience."

For three hours she lay there in the bed, watching her mother's breathing, and when it happened, she knew. She knew she had seen her mother's last breath. "I have never experienced anything more painful," she told me. "I loved her so much." She told me she was disappointed that she hadn't had a spiritual experience.

Breathing in the Spirit

There are breathing prayers in many spiritual traditions. The Torah teaches that God breathed the breath of life into Adam's nostrils (Gn 2:7) and the rabbis teach that we should praise God with every breath we take (*Bereshit Rabba,* 14, end). After the resurrection, when Jesus appears to his disciples, he breathes on them, saying, "Receive the Holy Spirit" (Jn 20:22). Breath is both life and spirit.

Begin by breathing slowly and deeply. Choose a prayer or passage from scripture that has special meaning for you, or you might say this prayer from the Morning Service:

O my God, the soul that you have given me is pure— you created it, you formed it, you breathed it into me, and you keep it within me. . . . And so, as long as my soul is within me, I will thank you and praise you, O Lord my God and the God of my fathers, Master of all actions, Lord of all souls.[18]

Pause after each phrase to inhale and exhale several times.

There are many variations to this breathing prayer. Anthony De Mello, S.J., suggested imagining that you are breathing in God as you inhale and letting go of sin and impurity as you exhale. You might wish to repeat a brief prayer or petition as you pray, such as "Lord have mercy" or "Be still, my soul." Yitzhak Buxbaum suggests simply meditating on God's love entering you as you inhale and your love going out to God as you exhale.[19] If you do this prayer regularly you will find that you can call on it whenever you are anxious or in pain, and it will have a calming, centering effect, connecting you to the Source of all love and strength.

Reading and Prayer

Now there was a great wind, so strong that it was splitting mountains and breaking rocks in pieces before the LORD, but the LORD was not in the wind; and after the wind an earthquake, but the LORD was not in the earthquake; and after the earthquake a fire, but the LORD was not in the fire; and after the fire a sound of sheer silence. When Elijah heard it, he wrapped his face in his mantle and went out and stood at the entrance of the cave (1 Kgs 19:11-13).

Dear God, how often we do not see you because we are expecting something else, something loud or big or awesome or other-worldly. And yet, you are in the silence, the gentle breath, the embrace, the chuckle, even the pain. You are as unseen and yet as necessary as the air we breathe. You have hallowed our humanity. Help us to listen. Teach us to recognize your voice. And enliven us, breath of God, with your eternal life.

ELEVEN

The Shoebox

My friend Paul told me this story about his friend Al. Al was one of those people one sometimes sees at AA meetings who stay sober for a few weeks, go out, get drunk, disappear for a month or two, and reappear, looking the worse for wear. Al was the kind of guy who helps everyone else stay sober. You'd start thinking about taking a drink, and then you'd think about Al and you'd say to yourself, "Nope, it's just not worth it." None of the other recovering alcoholics were surprised that Al drank—it was easy for a fellow alcoholic to understand that. What was truly impressive was that Al kept coming back, over and over again. Why couldn't Al stay sober? His AA friends told him he needed the spiritual side of the program, but Al hated "God talk." He didn't believe in any Higher Power, and he didn't want to either. He just wanted to stay sober so he could get his life back together, and maybe reconcile with his long-suffering wife.

There's no telling how many times Al relapsed, but finally there came a day when he decided that he would try that "spiritual stuff." He was told he could choose his own Higher Power, not someone else's idea of God, but God as Al understood him, her, or it. So Al chose his Higher Power. Al chose a shoebox.

No one at the meetings so much as raised an eyebrow. "Your Higher Power is a shoebox? Okay, Al, just keep coming back," they said. Al took his shoebox with him everywhere he went: in his car, to the office, to meetings, to the grocery store, even to the ball game. In the morning Al would ask the shoebox to keep him sober. During the day when he felt like drinking he would ask the shoebox to help him not take that first drink. At night he would thank the shoebox for his sobriety. And Al stayed sober. The shoebox became old and worn, but Al continued to carry it with him wherever he went. Al began to look healthier and happier. He got a job and a haircut. He started paying off old bills, even back taxes. He made friends, real friends not just bar buddies. And he stayed sober.

One day Al came to his meeting without his shoebox. His AA friends asked him, "You okay, Al?" Al replied, "Sure, I feel fine." He certainly looked good. "But your shoebox," his friends asked him, "what happened to your shoebox?" Al shrugged, and said, "I figured there was no point in carrying around something that was already here."

Searching for God

Some of us grew up with great faith in our ideas about God and some of us grew up with no idea of God at all. Ultimately, most of us come to the same moment in our lives when whatever idea of God we have proves inadequate in the face of our life experience. When we are suffering or someone we love is suffering, we may find our old ideas of God lacking or feel a need for a faith we never had. Some of us get angry. Some of us become disillusioned. Some of us look for another god to fill the emptiness. Some of us give up on God. Some of us begin seeking God, but don't know where to look. The following is an approach to prayer, sometimes suggested in AA, which acknowledges our human limitations while staying open to the possibility of God's presence.

Choose a "shoebox." Your shoebox could be anything: a stone, a medal, an empty bowl. Your shoebox isn't God. It's simply a reminder to talk to God and an acknowledgment that we are praying to God, not to our inadequate concept of God. It is an attempt to give God space to reveal God's self to us in unexpected ways. Choose something you can take with you wherever you go. Place it beside your bed at night. In the morning focus on your "shoebox" and ask for guidance to do God's will that day. When you are tempted to do something you know is wrong, focus on your "shoebox" and ask God to help you do what is right. At night, thank your "shoebox" for helping you. Use your "shoebox" until you begin to experience God's presence in your life throughout the day. Notice, I didn't say until you *feel* God's presence or until you *understand* God's presence.

Feelings and understandings about God can be helpful, but they are not always necessary, and when we are in pain they may not be accessible. Al knew that God was present because he was able to live a healthier and holier life when he talked to his Higher Power than when he didn't. Whether or not we *feel* God's presence, we know we are *experiencing* God's presence when we are empowered to do what is right and good.

Reading and Prayer

Where can I go from your spirit? Or where can I flee from your presence? If I ascend to heaven, you are there; if I make my bed in Sheol, you are there. If I take the wings of the morning and settle at the farthest limits of the sea, even there your hand shall lead me, and your right hand shall hold me fast. If I say, "Surely the darkness shall cover me, and the light around me become night," even the darkness is not dark to you; the night is as bright as the day, for darkness is as light to you (Ps 139:7-12).

By what name shall I call you, Incomprehensible Spirit, Mother God, Creator of All that is Good, Breath of Life, Eternal Word? My words cannot speak you. My thoughts are so small they cannot contain you. If you are, you are not a comfortable God, not an easy God to love. I want a smaller god whose ways I understand, whose will I can bend to mine. But you, Infinite Power, who am I to love you? How am I to love you? And yet, without you I am an empty shell, a dry riverbed, a skeleton. Therefore I call on you because I must.

There is no one else to whom I can turn for so great a need. I call to you in words I cannot understand. I call to you from my silence when I am weary of words. Answer me. Fill my emptiness, flood my dryness, clothe my bones, shine in my darkness, and love me, love me, love me, that I may love you.

TWELVE

A Bit o' Brot

My friend, Leah, was a baby in her mother's womb when the concentration camp at Auschwitz was liberated and her mother freed. Leah told me that she had once asked her mother how she had survived the horrors of the camp. Her mother told her this story:

The prisoners were not given enough to eat. There was no one who was not hungry, but there was a man sicker and weaker than herself. She knew that he could not survive long on the little food he was given. Although her own portion was meager, she decided to save a bit of her own bread to give to this man. It was not an easy thing to do. She had to hide the bread and then sneak it to the man, knowing that if she were caught she would be killed. Each day she would think about how best to save and hide this bit o' brot, as she called it, to give to the sickly man. Each day, somehow, she found a way. And she lived, a day at a time, through unspeakable suffering. It was not the food she ate that kept her alive, she said, but that little bit o' brot she gave away.

Finding God Through Giving

It has long been a tradition in Jewish homes to have a box in which one saved money to give to the poor. Even poor people kept a box, for the tradition recognizes that we all have something to give. It was the practice to put something in this box before praying.

Giving not only brings justice to the earth but it opens our hearts to receive our God more fully. We give not only because others need our gifts but because we need to be givers. Often when we are sick or suffering it is easy to think we have little to give. We lack our former strength. We may feel useless and worry that we are a burden to others. It is important to realize that however weak or poor we may be, God continues to need us to make this world a more just place.

Use a box or other container that you can keep in a handy place—beside your bed, on your desk, or wherever you go to pray. Place whatever amount of money you are able to give into the box before you say your prayers. Later, give this money to someone in need.

You may wish to give more than money. Set a tablet and pen beside the box. Spend a few minutes becoming still and focused. Think about what you have to give others; not about what you used to be able to give, or what you might be able to give in the future, but what you have to give today. Perhaps you have a talent. Perhaps you could give of your time. Pay attention to the little things. A smile or a word of encouragement to a hardworking nurse if you're in the hospital, a prayer for someone who needs your prayers, and a postcard to someone who is lonely are all simple little gifts that can bring the light of God into the lives of others. Before you say your prayers, put something in the box. Put money into the giving box to give to the poor, but also write down and place in the box the other gifts you decide to give. Remember that your life is of infinite value. God needs you.

Reading and Prayer

Why do you spend your money for that which is not bread, and your labor for that which does not satisfy? Listen carefully to me, and eat what is good, and delight yourselves in rich food. Incline your ear, and come to me; listen, so that you may live. I will make with you an everlasting covenant, my steadfast, sure love for David. . . . For as the rain and the snow come down from heaven, and do not return there until they have watered the earth, making it bring forth and sprout, giving seed to the sower and bread to the eater, so shall my word be that goes out from my mouth; it shall not return to me empty, but it shall accomplish that which I purpose, and succeed in the thing for which I sent it (Is 55:2-3, 10-11).

Dear God, the bread we eat sustains our bodies, but the bread we give away sustains our souls, giving our lives meaning, purpose, and integrity even in the midst of unbearable and senseless suffering.

I hunger for fulfillment, but you feed me with desire.
I hunger for self-confidence, but you feed me with faith.
I hunger for security, but you feed me with hope.
I hunger for peace, but you feed me with longing.
I hunger for meaning, but you feed me with mystery.
I hunger for love, and you give me your people to love.
I thank you God for feeding my soul with hunger for you.

THIRTEEN

The Secret

Anna came to me for counseling because she was engaged to be married and knew that she must tell her fiancé a secret. It was something so terrible she did not like to think about it, let alone speak of it out loud. "I know I must tell him," she said, "for there must not be secrets between us." She instinctively knew that their love could only thrive in light, not in darkness, nurtured by trust, not fear. "If I tell him," she said, "he may not want me; but if I don't tell him, I will know that I never really trusted him." Not only did she fear he might reject her, she was concerned that he might feel burdened by her truth. She wanted someone to be there to support both of them when she made her disclosure. I thought perhaps she had committed some grievous sin, but, as it turned out, it was not her sin that plagued her. Rather, she had been the victim of another's sin. She told me, in a soft voice, with downcast eyes, of how her stepfather had molested her repeatedly when she was a child, and of how her mother had refused to believe her and failed to protect her.

For a couple of weeks Anna came to see me. It was the first time she had shared her secret. When she felt ready, she invited her fiancé to come with her. I knew it took courage for her to share her secret with this man she loved. By now, I had come to have considerable respect for Anna, and I hoped she had chosen a man worthy of her trust. He listened attentively, and when she was finished he got out of his chair, went to kneel beside her, and took her in his arms. For a long time they simply held each other. Her trust only deepened his love. His acceptance was healing for her. Anna had chosen well.

Anna continued to meet with me for several weeks after this. Having opened up with someone about her secret pain, she felt a need to talk about it and to explore the impact it had had on her. The better I got to know Anna, the more I wondered how a woman who had suffered so profoundly throughout her child-hood was able to live such a healthy, happy, productive life. Her experiences had affected her, yes, but they had not led her into sinfulness, self-destruction, self-pity, or despair. Her pain had neither hardened her nor warped her. It was clear to me that she had some deep inner reservoir of strength which sustained her.

"What has helped you deal with all this?" I asked her one day. "What is the source of your strength?" She answered without the slightest hesitation. "When I was a little girl," she said, "I had a dream. I dreamed that I was at the park playing with some other children. I saw a man in a wheelchair. He was having trouble going up the hill, and he called to me to help him. I went to him and I pushed his chair up the hill. When we got to the top, he thanked me, and as he spoke to me he looked at me. There was such tenderness and sweetness in his eyes." Anna's eyes filled with tears. "Never have I felt such love as I felt at that moment, but I didn't realize who he was. Then, in the dream, I was at a birthday party. There he was again, waiting for me to come to him. The other children at the party didn't seem to notice, but I saw the wounds in his hands and I knew that this man in the wheelchair was Jesus. I hurried up to him. 'Why have you come to me?' I asked him. 'Why did you ask *me* to push your chair?' Again he looked at me with indescribable sweetness. 'I came to you, Anna,' he said, 'because you need me.'"

When Anna finished her story, we sat in silence for a while. The love she had experienced in that moment seemed to flow out of her, filling the little room in which we sat. I, too, could feel it. "After that," she said, "I had only to remember the way he looked at me to know I was loved."

I have met many people who have received grace, but I have met no one who has made better use of their gift of grace than Anna. Throughout a difficult and painful life, she had returned again and again to feed on this morsel of love experienced only once in a child-hood dream. Fed by this moment of grace, she had grown up whole and healthy, able to love and be loved. I pray that I may learn to use the graces I receive half so well as Anna.

Letting God Love Us

Sometimes the simplest prayers are the best. This is especially true when you or someone you love is suffering. Lack of sleep, anxiety, pain, and the effects of medication may make it difficult to pray. Those who have experienced trauma may find that painful memories emerge when they are silent and alone with God. People often avoid praying in order to avoid these painful memories.

St. Teresa, a sixteenth-century mystic and Carmelite founder, suffered serious ill health for many years. At one point she wrote: "I have been experiencing now for three months such great noise and weakness in my head that I've found it a hardship even to write concerning necessary business matters."[20] Yet during this time of suffering she wrote one of the most sublime works on prayer ever written. This is an approach to prayer she recommended to her sisters. It is helpful for anyone who is in pain or suffering.

Begin with a few words of contrition, confessing whatever it is that is troubling your conscience and asking forgiveness. Make the sign of the cross. Now imagine the Lord in the room with you, sitting or standing beside you. Realize that he is present to you as your dearest friend and companion. Look on him humbly and lovingly and let him gaze on you. Simply be with him as long as you are able, and return to be with him as often as you can.

This prayer may take a few seconds or a few hours. The length of time is not as important as one's willingness to be open to the love of Jesus. Teresa tells us:

If you grow accustomed to having him present at your side, and he sees that you do so with love and that you go about striving to please him, you will not be able—as they say—to get away from him; he will never fail you; he will help you in all your trials; you will find him everywhere. Do you think it's some small matter to have a friend like this at your side?[21]

Reading and Prayer

"Come, you that are blessed by my Father, inherit the kingdom prepared for you from the foundation of the world; for I was hungry and you gave me food, I was thirsty and you gave me something to drink, I was a stranger and you welcomed me, I was naked and you gave me clothing, I was sick and you took care of me, I was in prison and you visited me" (Mt 25:34).

Almighty and all powerful God, you come to us as an infant and give your life for us, naked, thirsting, bleeding, and dying on a cross. It is in weakness and vulnerability, in suffering and neediness that you are most visible. And it is when we are hungry or thirsty, estranged or naked, sick, lonely, or imprisoned, that you are most present in us. Then let me not hold back. Open my heart to receive you as you come to me in the people I meet each day, even in the suffering I experience each day. Help me to see you in their faces and may they, dear God, ever see you in mine.

FOURTEEN

Communion

I was running late one day, and got to the unit to distribute communion moments after the dinner trays had arrived. I went into one woman's room. She was an elderly woman recovering from surgery on an arthritic knee. She had her tray on the table in front of her. She looked at the pyx in my hand and said, "Oh dear, I've just got my dinner. I'm afraid I'll need to wait until tomorrow to receive communion." I told her I would return the following day, and I went into the next room.

The man in this room was a middle-aged Italian mechanic who had suffered a back injury in an accident at work. He had also just received his dinner tray. "Oh, thank goodness," he said. "I haven't started to eat yet so I can receive communion." We prayed together and he received. I went to the next room.

There were two women in this room. One was diabetic and was having trouble with her eyes. The other was an older woman suffering from cancer. Once again the dinner trays had been set before the women, but they had not yet started to eat. The first woman saw me and cried out, clapping her hands joyfully, "This is wonderful! I shall eat dinner with Jesus!" The woman in the bed next to her said, "I wasn't raised Catholic, but my husband was Catholic and we raised our children Catholic. They are dead now, but when I see you with the host I feel that they are here with me." There were tears in her eyes.

Blessing One Another

This is a prayer that one does with another person. Ask someone you love and trust, who shares your faith in God, to share this prayer of blessing. The person who is giving the blessing places his or her hands on the other person's head. The person being blessed remains silent until the blessing is complete. You may wish to bless each other. It can be a powerful experience to have more than one person give the blessing. Each person in turn places his or her hands on the head of the person being blessed. Use your own words of blessing, or, if the person being blessed is suffering, you may wish to say:

God comforts us in all our afflictions.
Blessed be God forever.

The person being blessed responds:
Blessed be God forever.[22]

Reading and Prayer

"If you love me, you will keep my commandments. And I will ask the Father, and he will give you another Advocate, to be with you forever. This is the Spirit of truth, whom the world cannot receive, because it neither sees him nor knows him. You know him, because he abides with you, and he will be in you. I will not leave you orphaned; I am coming to you. In a little while the world will no longer see me, but you will see me; because I live, you also will live" (Jn 14:15-19).

Dear God, you do not always come to me in the same way. Sometimes I experience your majesty and mystery. Filled with awe, I take off my shoes in your presence. Sometimes you are my closest friend, nearer and dearer to me than any other. You embrace me. Sometimes I know you only through the love of others. It is through their caring that you are present to me. And then there are the dark days when you seem a stranger to me and I feel I am not able to receive you at all.

Sometimes you come at inconvenient times; you ask things of me I'm not sure I can do, and the people you give me to love are irritating, troublesome, and difficult to get along with. Sometimes I don't feel very good about myself. I wonder why you bother with me at all, and when you come to me I want to pull the covers over my head and hide. Help me not to hide from you. Help me to receive you whenever you come, however you come, in whomsoever you come that I might live in you and you in me, forever.

FIFTEEN

Dark Night

Sara was a happy person, happily living a rather ordinary life. She had a good-looking husband with an easygoing temperament, three healthy, active children, a well-trained dog, and two arrogant but elegant cats. There was in Sara's life, as there probably is in every life, something extra-ordinary. What was extra-ordinary about Sara was that she walked with Jesus. She had never had a vision, never felt a blinding sense of God's presence, but she lived her life with a constant, quiet, and very real sense that Jesus was walking beside her. She talked to him continuously about her joys and sorrows, her worries and achievements. She turned to him when she felt impatient with a sleepless child or anxious because her checkbook didn't balance. Always he was there, helping her when she needed help, forgiving her failures, loving her. She didn't talk about it with others, but she had shared once with a priest while on a weekend retreat. He had confirmed what she already knew—her friendship with Jesus was a special gift.

Then one day, a day like any other, this gift was gone. She turned to Jesus and he wasn't there. Of course she knew he was there really, but she had no sense of his presence. She tried to imagine him standing beside her, but couldn't. She tried reading scripture. She might as well have been reading the *Wall Street Journal*. She knew the words had meaning, they just didn't mean anything to her. She tried thinking about God, but her thoughts fell out of her head like sand through a sieve. She went to her favorite chapel where she had always experienced a sense of peace. She felt no peace, only a profound emptiness. She began to wonder if God didn't love her anymore, but she put that thought aside. Of course God loved her. Maybe she had done something wrong. Well of course she had. Her life was littered with the usual petty sins, but Jesus had always forgiven her and encouraged her to do better. She couldn't believe he would condemn her now. She prayed to be close to Jesus again, but the harder she prayed, the more distant she felt.

This emptiness and sense of distance was the most painful thing she had ever experienced. What made it worse was the simple fact that nothing was wrong. She had a good life, a happy marriage, a wonderful family, and work she enjoyed. What was the matter with her? Yet Sara knew that there was something profoundly wrong. She was in the deepest pain she had ever experienced, and it didn't help that no one knew. There were no sympathy cards, no vases of flowers, no words of encouragement. She started to feel sorry for herself, but Sara didn't approve of self-pity. She told herself not to be ridiculous.

Even though she no longer sensed his presence, Sara continued to talk to Jesus. She told him about her pain. She asked to be close to him. The more she tried to talk to him, the farther from him she felt. She went back to see the priest she had talked to on retreat and explained her difficulty. He told her that she was in a dark night and encouraged her to read a book by St. John of the Cross. This didn't help—the priest was talking to her as if she were a mystic, and she knew better. Dark nights were something saints went through, but she obediently bought the book and began to read it. Poetry! She was in no mood for poetry. She put the book away. Sara found that she no longer liked to pray, in fact, she hated to pray. Prayer only made her face this awful emptiness. But she was too stubborn to give up on prayer. Perhaps at the heart of her stubbornness was the hidden hope that Jesus would come back to her. So although she felt incapable of prayer, she kept on praying, "Come back to me."

Just as her friendship with Jesus had once infused her life with a sense of gratitude, her sense of emptiness now seeped into her life, making her feel dissatisfied with everything and everyone. Nothing was wrong, but everything was wrong. Her prayer to be close to God turned into a kind of spiritual whining, like a small child deprived of a favorite toy. "Why are you doing this to me?" she cried out, in the privacy of her heart. "I thought you loved me." It was then that she heard a voice within her saying, "But Sara, this is what you asked for." And she knew it was him. "No, Lord," she said, "I never asked for this." "Yes, Sara," she heard his voice clearly now, speaking from the core of her being. "You asked to be close to me," he said.

With those words her pain was transformed. This pain, this absence, this thirst for his presence became, itself, an experience of presence. The pain which had filled her with dissatisfaction now filled her with joy. Her thirst for God *was* God. And she knew this, not with her mind but with her soul. The experience lasted briefly, perhaps only a minute, but it left in its wake a deep peace-giving knowledge. She understood now that he had not left her. Rather, he was drawing her more deeply into himself.

Asking for Help

Jesus encourages us to call on God for help whenever we are in need. He tells us, "Ask, and it will be given you; search, and you will find; knock, and the door will be opened for you" (Mt 7:7). The problem most of us have is that we don't know *when* we are in need. We tend to associate need with crisis. "I need God's help when I am in a fix." The rest of the time we mistakenly think our own willpower will suffice. Nor do we know *what* we need. We think we need to be comfortable, happy, secure, successful, self-satisfied. It often seems to me that God doesn't see my needs the way I do.

In the famous scene when Jesus reprimands Martha for trying to get her sister to help with the chores, Jesus tells Martha, "Only one thing is needful." Her sister Mary, who has been sitting at his feet listening to him while Martha works away in the kitchen, has chosen "the better part." What is the one thing that is needful in my life? What is this "better part"? If I had to pick one thing, what would it be? Fame? Fortune? A perfect figure? A great marriage? Healthy children? How far up on my list of needs have I put my need for God?

If I know that I need God, and I need God continuously, how am I to get this need met? Jesus tells us to ask and it will be given to us. Is it really that simple?

One of my favorite writings on prayer was written by a fourth-century monk. In his treatise *The Conferences*, John Cassian shares wisdom gleaned from the early desert fathers and mothers. In one of his conferences on prayer (Conference Ten), Father Isaac tells

Cassian that anyone who wishes to keep awareness of God always in mind should cling to the words from Psalm 70, "Come to my help, O God; Lord, hurry to my rescue." He writes,

This verse, I say, is necessary and useful for each one of us in whatever condition we may live. For whoever desires to be helped always and in all things shows that he needs God as helper not only in hard and sad affairs but also and equally as much in favorable and joyful ones. . . .[23]

He proceeds to speak eloquently of the great variety of circumstances in which we may find ourselves in need of this prayer: when we want to eat too much, when we have a bad headache, insomnia, a temptation to some vice, or a temptation to be proud of our virtues.

The idea is to ask for God's help in everything throughout the day. When you get up in the morning and are beginning your day, pray, "Come to my help, O God, hurry to my rescue." When you are feeling impatient as you encounter rush hour traffic on the way to work, pray, "Come to my help, O God, hurry to my rescue." Throughout the day as you encounter good and ill, in every difficulty, every achievement, every mundane task, continue to pray, "Come to my help, O God, hurry to my rescue."

Do this as faithfully as you can for a day, or a week. No one will do it perfectly. Do the best you can. Notice what happens to your relationship with God. What happens to your life. What happens to you. I don't know what will happen for you, but I am confident that something good will happen. I believe Jesus meant it when he said, "Ask and you shall receive."

Reading and Prayer

But as for me, my prayer is to you, O Lord. At an acceptable time, O God, in the abundance of your steadfast love, answer me. With your faithful help rescue me from sinking in the mire; let me be delivered from my enemies and from the deep waters. Do not let the flood sweep over me, or the deep swallow me up, or the Pit close its mouth over me. Answer me, O Lord, for your steadfast love is good; according to your abundant mercy, turn to me. Do not hide your face from your servant, for I am in distress—make haste to answer me (Ps 69:13-17).

When I look at you, Jesus, I see your poverty.

I see how you, who were rich, for my sake became poor.

You were born of a young woman in a shed where animals were kept.

You were considered ordinary and unremarkable by your playmates,

criticized by your peers and abandoned by your friends.

You were scorned, beaten, stripped of dignity, and killed.

You were so poor, Jesus. I am afraid of this poverty

and yet I am drawn to it,

for I am drawn to you, Jesus.

How can I be truly close to you

if I do not embrace your poverty?

Come to my help, O God, hurry to my rescue,

for I am afraid to embrace so great a love as yours.

I do not know how to receive so great a gift as eternity.

SIXTEEN

The Rice Bowl

When I was a child, I wanted to be a missionary. This wasn't surprising as I come from seven generations of missionaries, ministers, and theologians. There were a lot of missionaries in my life. My father was on the National Board of Missions for the Presbyterian Church, and he brought the missions home with him in a steady stream of immigrants. My grandmother grew up on a Choctaw reservation where her father was a minister, and I had cousins in Africa who told wonderful stories whenever they came to visit. I was particularly fascinated by our neighbor, Topper, a lean young man with a serious expression and the engaging ability to take idealistic young girls as seriously as they took themselves. Topper always kept an empty bowl on his desk. He told me that it was to remind him of the hungry people of the world.

When Topper left for Africa to work with Dr. Schweitzer, I decided that I would become a medical missionary and travel to China. Why China? I don't know. I've always dreamed of the Orient. I saved my pennies and began sponsoring an orphan. The orphanage sent me pictures which I put up around my room. I decided I wanted a bowl like Topper's.

That Thanksgiving, we went to my Uncle John and Aunt Alberta's home for dinner. As we waited for the turkey to brown, I wandered into my uncle's study. On the shelf by his desk sat a black wooden bowl. I picked it up. It wasn't a very nice looking bowl. It was chipped and the inside was all scratched. I wondered why Uncle John kept it. My aunt was a fastidious housekeeper and their home always looked so neat. The old bowl seemed out of place. I picked it up to inspect it more closely. Just then, my uncle walked in.

"Do you like that bowl?" he asked. I thought about Topper and all the hungry people that needed to be fed.

"Yes," I said, intently. Uncle John sat down in the overstuffed chair beside me.

"That bowl was taken off the body of a Japanese soldier during the war," he said. " It's his rice bowl."

I looked at the scratches on the inside. "He made these scratches when he was eating?" I asked.

Uncle John nodded. "I keep it to remind me that our enemies are human. They get hungry just like we do. They have feelings and families. It's important to remember that." I looked up at him. I recognized the look on his face. My father got that same faraway look on the rare occasions when he talked about the war. We sat there awhile in silence. It was one of those magical childhood moments when you realize you've entered the adult world and suddenly find yourself standing shoulder to shoulder with someone you once stood on tiptoe to kiss. I knew that most of their friends had died in the war. Was he thinking about them? Or about the Japanese soldier? Had he taken the bowl or had someone given it to him? Had he killed someone? It was hard to imagine my uncle killing anyone. I'd never had an enemy. I wondered what it would be like to have to kill someone. Would I want to remember that?

"Do you want it?" he asked me. I couldn't believe he meant it.

"Yes," I said simply.

"Take it, then," he said. "I want you to have it. You will value it, and it should be valued." I had never felt more complimented.

"Thanks," I said, inadequately. I would keep it on a chest of drawers like Topper, and I would remember. I would remember the hungry and I would remember the Japanese soldier who had eaten rice, scraping the bottom of the bowl with his fingernails.

Years later, I heard that Topper had disappeared in Africa. He was last seen going downstream, bringing medical supplies to people who lived in an area approachable only by boat. My uncle and I never talked about the war again. And I never became a missionary. My husband proposed a few months before I was scheduled to go to China, so we got married and I went to Michigan instead. But the old rice bowl still sits in the corner of my office where I pray.

Most of us don't want to think about suffering, and we certainly don't want to remember it. But there is some healing that can only come if we are willing to remember the pain—others' pain and our own. Sometimes I hold the bowl in my hands and I remember. I remember all the pain I'd rather forget. And I pray. I pray for the hungry. I pray for peace. I pray that God will fill our emptiness with his presence. I pray for all the serious-eyed children who dream of doing something courageous and holy. And I pray with gratitude for those who nurture their dreams.

Praying for Our Enemies

My years as a therapist have given me an awareness of the infectious nature of evil. In war, in crime, in abuse, both perpetrator and victim are left scarred. This doesn't seem right. The victims, who have done no wrong, shouldn't feel guilty—but they do. They shouldn't feel ashamed—but they do. Their self-worth and freedom should not be diminished—but they are. Why is this? I believe it is because we truly are united, interconnected, interdependent. When my brother sins, my soul is wounded. When I sin, my sister suffers the effects. Unless we do something to counter its contagious effects, sin will breed sin: the abused become the abusers, the victims become the perpetrators. Praying for our enemies is an antidote to this spiritual poison. By praying for our enemies, we inoculate ourselves against the contagious effects of sin, against resentments, shame, hatred, and bitterness.

Who is my enemy? Anyone with whom I am angry or resentful becomes my enemy when I wish them ill. Anyone I want to hurt has become my enemy. These enemies may be people I fear or people I despise, people who have hurt me or people who simply irritate me; but if I wish them anything less than the fullness of God's love and forgiveness, it is my own heart which is choosing evil and my own heart which must change.

It is not necessary (or advisable) to wait until I feel forgiving to make an act of forgiveness by praying for my enemies, for Christ tells us clearly that as we forgive so shall we be forgiven. And who among us does not have much to be forgiven? To pray for our enemies is to will good in the face of evil, to ask our God, the source of all goodness, to set right what is wrong. When we cooperate with God's goodness in this way, we open the doors of our hearts to the healing power of God's love. The *Catechism of the Catholic Church* teaches that:

> It is not in our power not to feel or to forget an offense; but the heart that offers itself to the Holy Spirit turns injury into compassion and purifies the memory in transforming the hurt into intercession . . . forgiveness also bears witness that, in our world, love is stronger than sin (2843-2844).

Traditionally, we pray for our enemies before communion and before retiring in the evening. Some people picture the person being prayed for in their minds, others light a candle for each person being prayed for. You might pray in your own words or use the following prayer by St. Thomas More.

> Almighty God, have mercy on N. and N., and on all that bear me evil will, and would do me harm, and their faults and mine together by such easy, tender, merciful means as thine infinite wisdom best can devise, vouchsafe to amend and redress and make us saved souls in heaven together, where we may ever live and love together with Thee and Thy blessed saints, O glorious Trinity, for the bitter passion of our sweet Savior Christ. Amen.[24]

Reading and Prayer

In days to come the mountain of the LORD's house shall be established as the highest of the mountains, and shall be raised up above the hills. Peoples shall stream to it, and many nations shall come and say: "Come, let us go up to the mountain of the LORD, to the house of the God of Jacob; that he may teach us his ways and that we may walk in his paths." For out of Zion shall go forth instruction, and the word of the LORD from Jerusalem. He shall judge between many peoples, and shall arbitrate between strong nations far away; they shall beat their swords into plowshares, and their spears into pruning hooks; nation shall not lift up sword against nation, neither shall they learn war any more; but they shall all sit under their own vines and under their own fig trees, and no one shall make them afraid; for the mouth of the LORD of hosts has spoken (Mi 4:1-4).

———————— 🪰 ————————

Holy God, source of all peace,
cleanse my mind of all resentments
and my heart of all anger.
Help me to desire only goodness,
even toward those who have harmed me.
Teach me how to forgive so that,
believing in the power of your love,
I may be able to receive your forgiveness.
I ask this through Christ our Lord. Amen.

———————— 🪰 ————————

SEVENTEEN

The Beads

Gail was not good at being sick. She was an active, take charge sort of person who had reared eight children while running a local charity, with the efficiency of a top executive. When the youngest finally left the nest, she channeled her enormous energy into a small business. No one who knew her was surprised when the business became a smashing success. Now in her late seventies, Gail talked about "retiring someday"; but it was just talk, until the day she slipped on the ice and landed in a Chicago hospital with a broken hip.

I first met Gail when a nurse called the chaplain's office in desperation, hoping to find a rosary for Gail, whose own rosary had inadvertently been sent to the laundry along with her bed sheets. I didn't understand the nurse's tone of urgency until I met Gail. When I arrived at Gail's room, with a plastic rosary in hand, I discovered her drafting a long letter to the hospital administration about the numerous signs of incompetence she had observed during her hospital stay. Gail received the plastic rosary graciously. I noticed that her list of complaints contained many astute and accurate observations. It didn't take long to realize that I was dealing with a mature, capable, and deeply frustrated woman. Gail was not accustomed to feeling powerless. She hated feeling powerless.

"I won't mind dying," she told me. "I've lived a good life and I believe in heaven. But this doing nothing is driving me crazy." Gail's life had always impacted the lives of others. Now, her exasperation was driving everyone around her crazy. I liked Gail. Perhaps I recognized in her the driving work ethic that characterized my own family. I made a habit of visiting with her and learned much about her children and grandchildren, her employees and neighbors. It became clear to me that not only was Gail a bright, driven, energetic woman, she was also a "people person." That is, she was focused on people, not on things or achievements. Gail spent a lot of time in the patient sitting room and often knew as much about the conditions of her fellow patients as their nurses. She knew who visited whom, what medications everyone was taking, and what kind of physical therapy they were receiving.

One day Gail was sharing her concern about a young brain-injured woman who had come onto the unit. The woman was in a coma. This distressed Gail.

"I want to *do* something," Gail told me. "Can't somebody *do* something to help that poor girl?" The truth is, there wasn't a whole lot anyone could do, except wait and hope that she would regain consciousness.

"We can pray for her," I said. It seemed a weak response. Prayer doesn't feel like doing, but I knew in my own heart that prayer has power and it was the one thing we could do. Gail's face lit up.

"Of course," she said, "how stupid of me! I'm ashamed of myself for not thinking of it sooner. I should be saying a novena!"

I'm not a cradle Catholic and, having entered the church after Vatican II, I had not had much exposure to Marian devotions. I have to admit that, at the time I met Gail, I had never even said a novena. Gail's enthusiasm ignited my convert curiosity.

Gail began her novena that night. The young girl for whom she was praying never left her room, so Gail relied on my daily visits for an update on her progress. Unfortunately, there was none. This didn't phase Gail. Although there was no change in the unconscious girl, it would be wrong to say that nothing was happening. Clearly, something was happening to Gail. She became calmer, less irritable, more cheerful. Once again she had found a cause worthy of her energy and, giving herself to it with the focus and enthusiasm that had made her a memorable force amongst family and employees, she was happy again.

If the change in Gail had been the only grace received through her prayers, in my mind, it would have been cause for rejoicing. But it was not the only grace. On the ninth day of Gail's novena, the young girl regained consciousness. She was on the road to recovery. Gail received this wonderful news not with the satisfaction I had expected, but with a tearful humility I had never seen in her before.

"You would think," she told me, "that after all my years of prayer and going to Mass, I would have had more faith. I wanted to believe, I really did, but in my heart, I doubted that God could use an old woman like me. I see now that falling on that ice was a blessing. It gives me time to pray for others and that's what God wants of me now."

Gail went at her new vocation with the same commitment she had brought to all her life's work. She wrote the names of family, friends, and fellow patients in a little book and prayed for them each day. She even took to highlighting names in the newspaper of people who needed prayers and added these to her book.

The day she left the hospital, I said to her, "I hope you have my name in that book of yours."

"Oh yes, honey," she assured me, "your name's on the first page."

In difficult times, I take comfort in knowing that Gail is out there, somewhere, praying for me. I am grateful for her prayers, but I am also grateful that she introduced me to the novena. It is one of the great graces of my life that the people I try to help so often end up helping me. They open doors I wouldn't have thought to try and invite me into rooms of prayer and healing I might not have entered otherwise.

We live in a cynical age. We believe in facts, not in miracles. Sometimes our cynicism gets in our way. It keeps us from hoping for, from willing and working for the good. I do not know how God will answer my prayers. I do not pretend that the Almighty is somehow under my control. Like Gail, I am often surprised when my prayers are answered, and I am painfully aware, at these moments, of my lack of faith. But I do believe, and I truly want to believe, that if I persist in seeking the goodness of God, God will answer my prayers with a wondrous overflowing of love and grace.

Praying the Rosary

After the ascension of Jesus into heaven, Mary and the disciples gathered together to pray for the coming of the Holy Spirit, promised by Jesus. On the ninth day, Pentecost, their prayers were answered and the church was born. This is the origin of novenas, prayers said for nine days for a particular intention. Often these novena prayers are said in combination with the praying of the rosary.

The rosary evolved in the Middle Ages as a popular substitute for the Liturgy of the Hours. St. Dominic encouraged the devotion as an accessible and effective way for Christians to ponder the joyful, sorrowful, and glorious mysteries of the life of Jesus. There are many variations on the rosary: the seven dolor, the scriptural rosary, the five wounds rosary, and the Brigittine rosary, to name a few. The mysteries are traditionally divided into three groups of five each: The Joyful Mysteries (Annunciation, Visitation, Nativity, Presentation in the Temple, Finding in the Temple); the Sorrowful Mysteries (Agony in the Garden, Scourging at the Pillar, Crowning With Thorns, Carrying the Cross, Crucifixion); and the Glorious Mysteries (Resurrection, Ascension, Descent of the Holy Spirit, Assumption of Mary, Coronation of Our Lady).

The rosary begins with the Apostles' Creed, followed by the Lord's Prayer and three Hail Marys. Each decade consists of ten Hail Marys proceeded by the Lord's Prayer and followed by the Glory Be. The rosary is concluded with the Hail, Holy Queen prayer. It is customary to meditate on the Joyful Mysteries on Mondays, Thursdays, and the Sundays of Advent; the

Sorrowful Mysteries are prayed on Tuesdays, Fridays, and the Sundays of Lent; and the Glorious Mysteries are prayed on Wednesdays, Saturdays, and the remaining Sundays of the year.

The most helpful guidance I have received in praying the rosary comes from Pope John XXIII. In his Apostolic Letter on the Rosary, Pope John writes: "Every decade of Hail Marys has its own picture and every picture has a threefold character which is always the same: *mystical contemplation, private reflection,* and *pious intention.*" As we *contemplate* the mysteries, we commune in thought and feeling with the teaching and life of Jesus represented in the mystery. Then, as we *reflect* on this mystery with the guidance of the Holy Spirit, we confront our own lives, finding in each mystery the teaching which pertains to our lives and our own spiritual growth. Finally, we bring to this prayer our *intentions*, with personal prayers of intercession for our families, our friends, our neighbors, our church, our world. Pope John writes:

> *In this way the rosary becomes a world-wide supplication of individual souls and of the immense community of the redeemed, who from all parts of the world meet in a single prayer, either in private petitions imploring graces for each one's personal needs, or in sharing in the immense and general chorus of the whole Church praying for the supreme interests of [humankind].*[25]

Hail Mary

Hail Mary, full of grace, the Lord is with thee. Blessed art thou among women and blessed is the fruit of thy womb, Jesus. Holy Mary, Mother of God, pray for us sinners, now and at the hour of our death. Amen.

Glory Be

Glory be to the Father, and to the Son, and to the Holy Spirit. As it was in the beginning, is now, and ever shall be, world without end. Amen.

Hail, Holy Queen

Hail! Holy Queen, Mother of Mercy, our life, our sweetness, and our hope. To thee do we cry, poor banished children of Eve. To thee do we send up our sighs, mourning and weeping in this valley of tears. Turn then, most gracious advocate, thine eyes of mercy toward us; and after this our exile, show unto us the blessed fruit of thy womb, Jesus. O clement, O loving, O sweet Virgin Mary! Pray for us, O holy Mother of God, that we may be made worthy of the promises of Christ. Amen.

Apostles' Creed

I believe in God, the Father almighty, creator of heaven and earth. I believe in Jesus Christ, his only Son, our Lord. He was conceived by the power of the Holy Spirit and born of the Virgin Mary. He suffered under Pontius Pilate, was crucified, died, and was buried. He descended to the dead. On the third day he rose again. He ascended into heaven, and is seated at the right hand of the Father. He will come again to judge the living and the dead. I believe in the Holy Spirit, the holy catholic church, the communion of saints, the forgiveness of sins, the resurrection of the body, and the life everlasting. Amen.

Reading and Prayer

And Mary said,
"My soul magnifies the Lord,
and my spirit rejoices in God my Savior,
for he has looked with favor on the lowliness of his
    servant.
Surely, from now on all generations will call me
    blessed;
for the Mighty One has done great things for me,
and holy is his name.
His mercy is for those who fear him
from generation to generation.
He has shown strength with his arm;
he has scattered the proud in the thoughts of their
    hearts.
He has brought down the powerful from their
    thrones,
and lifted up the lowly;
he has filled the hungry with good things,
and sent the rich away empty.
He has helped his servant Israel,
in remembrance of his mercy,

according to the promise he made to our ancestors, to Abraham and to his descendants forever" (Lk 1:46-53).

Holy and All-powerful God,
I do not doubt your existence.
I look at the work of your hands
and I believe, O God, in you.
But that you should notice me and cherish me,
this is too wonderful to believe.
Give me a pure heart and a trusting soul, O God,
that I might believe in your incomprehensible love.

Eighteen

Homing Pigeon

Paul had no memory of the first eleven years of his life. He wanted to remember. He had looked at old family albums and tried to see what he must have seen back then, but he couldn't remember. He had been to therapists. He kept dream journals. He even went to group therapy. He hated group therapy. But he couldn't remember. He grieved for the lost memory as one would grieve for a twin.

At the same time he feared remembering. He knew what had happened. His brother had told him all about his alcoholic father who had beat them and then run off with his best friend's wife. He didn't remember the beatings, didn't want to; but he very much wanted to remember playing baseball in second grade and going to Yellowstone. He wanted to remember his first grade teacher. Most of all, he wanted to remember his father's face.

Paul left home to go to college when he was eighteen, and that's when it happened. He was taking a class called Psychology and Literature. The professor was a strange man with a thick German accent and bushy white hair. He was talking about the images in Hansel and Gretel, and how they represented the id and superego. As he spoke about the sexual significance of the dove, he cupped his hands as if he were holding a small bird. Suddenly Paul saw his own hands holding a homing pigeon. Then he saw his first grade friend, Michael. They were in Michael's garage where Michael's father kept his pigeons in tall wooden cages. Paul could see the bird sitting in his hands. It was soft and trembled as he held it.

Paul held his breath, treasuring the memory, willing it to last; but it evaporated. He sat through the rest of the class in a daze. He couldn't think about anything but the memory, his first memory from those first eleven years. But what a strange thing to remember! When he'd thought about remembering his life, he'd always assumed he would first remember his father's drunken rages that had left the family quaking long after he was gone. With a mixture of relief and disappointment, he realized that he hadn't remembered his father.

In the next few months, Paul's memories began to return, tumbling after each other. He shared them with his counselor, clinging to each memory like a long lost relative, afraid it would disappear. It was exhilarating and terrifying. He remembered the yelling and being pulled out of bed at three in the morning to be thrown onto the floor. He remembered trying to protect his mother with a baseball bat. Some of the memories made him break out in a sweat. Others made him want to vomit. They came in waves, but the memory he kept going back to was the memory of the bird.

He remembered how he and Michael had carried the bird out of the garage and into the open air. Michael had shown him how to hold his hands to release the bird. It had quivered in his hand, hesitant, and then spread its wings and flown into the sky. They had stared after it, wondering how far it would fly before it found its way home. The traumatic memories sickened him, but they passed. This memory stayed with him. Why?

One day his therapist said to him, "How do you feel when you remember holding that bird?"

"I feel safe," he said, "as if nothing can hurt me."

"What makes you safe?" his therapist asked.

Paul hadn't known he knew the answer until she asked the question, but now he knew. "It's God," he said. "It's as if God is holding me like I held that bird. It's why he let me have that memory first, so I'd know he is holding me." And then Paul understood. His father wasn't the man who had awakened him in the middle of the night and thrown him onto the floor. His father was the one who held him as gently as he had once held the homing pigeon. His father wanted him to be safe and free. With all his heart, Paul longed to see his father's face.

Telling Our Story

The spiritual practice of telling one's story exists in many spiritual traditions. From the earliest days of Christian monasticism, when young monks were encouraged to bear their souls to their spiritual fathers, to the storytelling practiced by today's Twelve Step fellowships, the practice of telling one's story has been used to help people grow spiritually. The process of telling our story to a loving listener can help us hear our own story in a new light. We glean fresh insights. Our listener may help us see things we cannot see ourselves. Increased understanding, however, is only one of the benefits of storytelling.

We are inclined, when faced with a problem in ourselves or others, to figure it out and try to fix it; but not all suffering can be understood or fixed. Then what? Too often when problem-solving fails, suffering people are left to fend for themselves. Their suffering is compounded by their isolation. Often what we need most to help us in our healing is simply to have others be present to us and hear us. The untold and secret parts of ourselves become interior islands on which self-doubt, fear, and even self-hatred breed. When we share a part of our story with an empathetic listener, we are affirmed. Light is cast on the darkest corners of self, and what was once despised, neglected, and unloved within us can be accepted, forgiven, loved, and healed.

Often, when we are in physical, psychological, or spiritual pain, pieces of our past will float to the surface. Somehow the present crisis recalls past experiences. As we share these with another, the past and present become more integrated. The acceptance and integration we experience can have a profoundly healing effect.

To tell your story, begin by writing down some of the thoughts, memories, and feelings that are coming up for you. Reflect on how these are connected. Ask God to help you see your experience in the light of God's love and truth. Then invite a close and trusted friend, chaplain, minister, or counselor to listen to your story. Let them know that you don't need them to solve your problems, but simply to listen. Choose a place and time when you can be comfortable, private, and uninterrupted. Be honest and open, seeking, as best you can, neither approval nor pity. Begin and end this storytelling time by praying together.

Reading and Prayer

This is the message we have heard from him and proclaim to you, that God is light and in him there is no darkness at all. If we say that we have fellowship with him while we are walking in darkness, we lie and do not do what is true; but if we walk in the light as he himself is in the light, we have fellowship with one another, and the blood of Jesus his Son cleanses us from all sin (1 Jn 1:5-7).

Eternal Light,

I am afraid of what I will have to face if I invite you into every dark corner of my mind and heart. I do not want to feel my loneliness and hurt. I do not want to remember my sins. Give me the courage to open the doors of my heart to your divine radiance. Conquer my fear of your love, even as the sun conquers the night, that I might walk in the light.

NINETEEN

The Blessing

Antonio's mother brought Antonio and his younger brother to counseling not long after their father had moved out. Antonio was ten and big for his age, while his brother was a thin, wiry six-year-old. Their father was an angry, immature, controlling man, who had beaten his wife and intimidated his children throughout their young lives. Antonio had been a quiet, obedient kid until Dad moved out; but then everything changed.

"I don't know what is the matter with him," his mother said. "I think he misses his father and he's angry; but he has to learn, he can't keep hitting his brother like this." Antonio had taken to slugging his younger brother with ever increasing frequency, had started getting into fights at school, and even kicked the family's pet cat. His mother was a bright, caring woman who loved her children, but the demands of trying to care for her children while going back to work, supporting her family, and fighting a nasty legal battle for child support left her depleted. Not surprisingly, she was finding it difficult to cope with a very angry ten-year-old.

Antonio was angry, all right. He was angry that his father had left. Angry that his mother was away at work so much. Angry that he'd had to change schools. He was now the man of the house, and he was dealing with his anger in the way his father had taught him, in the only way he knew. We began working with Antonio, trying to teach him healthier ways of dealing with his anger. We tried a number of things, but what proved most helpful was showing Antonio how to redirect his anger. When he wanted to hit his brother or kick the cat, he was encouraged to hit his pillow, bed, or stuffed animal instead. Antonio did not find either the pillow or the bed to be satisfying substitutes, but when his mother bought him a large stuffed bear to beat up, Antonio started making progress. Whenever he was angry he would go into his room and beat up his bear. The bear grew squishy and tattered, while Antonio started doing better at school. He got along better with the other kids, and though he fought with his brother, he quit hurting him. Once again, the family cat started sleeping on his bed. Antonio's mother was proud of him. So was I. Not surprisingly, Antonio became very attached to his bear, which he continued to hit whenever he was angry. The bouts of anger became less frequent, occurring most often when his mother had to work late or when he came back from a weekend with his father.

One day Antonio's mom came in to see me. She was laughing. "I have to tell you," she said, "it's so funny, but I'm a little worried."

"About Antonio?" I asked.

"Yes," she said. "It's about his bear. You know, the big one I got him to hit." She told me about how her local parish had had a special blessing ceremony. Parishioners were invited to receive a blessing, and to bring anything they wanted to have blessed. At the service, the priest had blessed Antonio, his brother, and his mom. Antonio had brought his bear to be blessed as well, and the priest had readily blessed the ragged bear.

"That's nice," I said, "he's very attached to that bear. But why are you worried?"

"Yesterday," his mother explained, "Antonio got really mad at his brother for ruining his drawing. I told him to go hit his bear, not his brother, but he said he couldn't hit his bear. He said that now that his bear has been blessed, it's holy and he can't hit it anymore." She laughed.

"Did you remind him that his brother was also blessed?" I asked.

"Oh yes," she said. "He says we're all holy now." She paused and added thoughtfully, "I wonder if the priest would be willing to bless our cat." She debated about whether or not to get him another stuffed animal, but decided to take a wait-and-see attitude.

I admit that I expected trouble. I thought Antonio would slug his brother or a kid at school. Afterall, most of us find it easy to forget that we are blessed. But Antonio surprised me. He kept out of trouble at school, yelled at his brother but refrained from hitting, and made the honor roll. Certainly the changes at home helped. Without his angry father at home, family life became more peaceful. His mother grew happier and more rested. The teachers at his new school were nurturing, and now that he wasn't hitting, he made friends more easily. His mother, telling me of his progress, informed me that Antonio had even started serving as an altar boy at their parish.

"An altar boy," his mother said. "Can you believe it?" I could readily believe it. Antonio seemed to have a natural spiritual aptitude, and I wasn't surprised that he was drawn to the church. Afterall, he had readily understood what so many of us struggle to take in—that through God's gift of grace we are, indeed, holy. And anything or anyone who is holy must be treated with love and respect. Even a holy bear.

Giving Thanks

One of the healing stories from the gospels which has always intrigued me is the story of the leper who returned to give thanks. In Luke 17:11-19, we hear how Jesus cleanses ten lepers, but only one, a Samaritan, returns to thank him. Jesus remarks on the fact that only one of the ten returned to "give praise to God" and says to him, "Get up and go on your way; your faith has made you well." It is not enough to be cleansed of bodily illness. True healing is a healing of the whole person which can only occur when, through faith, we enter into relationship with our God. It is in giving thanks that the leper enters into relationship.

Today, we tend to think of thanksgiving only in terms of gratitude; but in the Judeo-Christian tradition, thanksgiving is much more. Blessing and thanksgiving are closely related. The Hebrew word for blessing, *berakah*, is often translated as "thanksgiving." Christian *eucharistia*, or prayers of thanksgiving (the antecedents of our eucharist), are rooted in the Jewish prayers of blessing (*berakhot*). Early *eucharistia*, like the *berakah*, were not just an expression of gratitude but a declaration of faith in a God who has entered into relationship with us. This is the way in which Jesus himself gives thanks before raising Lazarus from the dead, saying, "Father, I thank you for having heard me. I knew that you always hear me, but I have said this for the sake of the crowd standing here, so that they may believe that you sent me" (Jn 11:41-42). Jesus gives thanks *before* God answers his prayer because for Jesus thanksgiving is not simply an expression of gratitude for receiving something desired but an acknowledgment of relationship, an expression of his faith that God, his Father, hears him.

In giving thanks, like the tenth leper, we enter into relationship with our Healer. Our healing has revealed to us that we are in relationship with a loving God who knows us and hears us. And now that we know who God is, we want to return to God, to speak to God, to be with God. Having experienced what this Healer can do for us, we want to tell others. We forget ourselves in our need to praise and glorify this God who loves us so deeply. This kind of thanksgiving takes us beyond the healing of our bodies and into the healing of our whole person. St. Paul tells us to "give thanks in all circumstances; for this is the will of God in Christ Jesus for you" (1 Thes 5:18).

Most of us, when we are confronted with illness or suffering, turn naturally to prayers of petition, seeking healing from our God. Yet there is great healing available to us through prayers of thanksgiving. St. Francis maintained that "The devils cannot harm the servant of Christ when they see he is filled with holy joy."[26] A heart that is overflowing with gratitude for God's goodness will not readily give in to temptation. Such a heart is open to the healing power of God's love.

John Cassian, in his Ninth Conference on prayer, says that prayers of thanksgiving are "begotten from considering God's benefits and his greatness and loving kindness." To turn our hearts and minds to praise and thanksgiving, we can begin by consciously remembering those times in our lives when we have experienced grace and love, healing or forgiveness; by recalling those moments when the beauty of creation has stirred our hearts to praise. If you have trouble remembering your blessings, ask God to help you remember moments of grace. Try writing down some of these memories in a gratitude journal to read on days when you are feeling dejected or out of touch with God. Treasuring these blessings, these experiences of grace, and reliving them in our thoughts is a powerful antidote to depression, anger, cynicism, and self-centeredness.

After spending time remembering these moments of grace in your life, say a prayer of thanksgiving. Use your own words or a traditional prayer of thanksgiving, such as the fourth-century hymn *Te Deum* ("You Are God"), or a psalm of thanksgiving. Read Psalm 92, which begins, "It is good to give thanks to the LORD, to sing praises to your name, O Most High; to declare your steadfast love in the morning, and your faithfulness by night . . . ," or Psalm 136 which begins, "O give thanks to the LORD, for he is good, for his steadfast love endures forever."

Reading and Prayer

I give you thanks, O Lord, with my whole heart; before the gods I sing your praise; I bow down toward your holy temple and give thanks to your name for your steadfast love and your faithfulness; for you have exalted your name and your word above everything. On the day I called, you answered me, you increased my strength of soul (Ps 138:1-3).

I give thanks to you, O God, for I know that you love me.

You are my Father who breathed life into me.

I thank you for my life.

You are the Son who died to save me.

I thank you for my salvation.

You are the Holy Spirit who helps me in every affliction.

I thank you for your comfort.

Although I fail again and again to be the person I long to be,

although at times life seems a burden and I grow discouraged,

still I will not lose heart.

I will not give up

for I know that your steadfast love endures forever.

Always and everywhere I will give thanks to you, O God,

for I know that you love me.

The Healing Way

As a child I used to have a recurring nightmare. I dreamed there was an open grave filled with living bodies, young and old, suffering and dying. The sky was black and filled with an acrid, choking smoke which burned my nostrils and throat. In the dream, my grandmother had been thrown into this open grave, and I longed go to her and pull her out of the grave; but soldiers, tall, broad shouldered men, towered over me and I was afraid. I stood, paralyzed, unable to move and hating myself for it. I always awoke from this dream weeping. Looking back on it, I think I must have heard stories of the Holocaust and known somehow, although it was never discussed, that my grandmother's people were Jewish. In my own mind, this open grave filled with living bodies became an inner image of suffering.

Years later, I had another dream. I dreamed I was on top of a green mountain. The skies were clear and the mountain was bathed in brilliant light. Suddenly the earth shook and the mountaintop split open. Inside were hundreds of crying, screaming people. It was the open grave of my childhood nightmares. I looked up, and on the other side of this pit of suffering I saw Jesus standing very still, looking at me with great love. I understood that I must descend into this suffering if I was to go to him. I was afraid, but my heart told me that if I did not turn from his intense and loving gaze, I would be safe. Being young, naive, and full of myself, I thought that God must be calling me to help these people, to bring them to God. I did not understand then that it was they who would carry me.

We do not seek suffering, for there is no goodness in it apart from God; but neither should we avoid suffering, either our own suffering or the suffering of others. Rather, we embrace the suffering that comes to us in our own lives and in the lives of our sisters and brothers, allowing it, through prayer, to be joined to love. As Christians, we believe that the way of the cross is our path to God. Sometimes we talk about carrying our crosses as if we each had our own cross to bear, but there is only one cross. It is on this cross that our isolation and divisions are healed, for the way of the cross is always a way to wholeness and unity. We seek God in our own suffering and in the suffering of others, knowing that, when joined to his infinite grace and love, all suffering leads to peace and healing.

NOTES

1. Joseph Cardinal Bernardin, *The Gift of Peace*, Chicago: Loyola Press, 1997, p. 99.

2. Michael Casey, *Toward God: The Ancient Wisdom of Western Prayer*, Liguori, MO: Triumph Books, 1996, p. 8.

3. Kieran Kavanaugh, O.C.D., and Otilio Rodriguez, O.C.D. *The Collected Works of St. Teresa of Avila*, vol. II. Washington, DC: Institute of Carmelite Studies, 1980, p. 291.

4. Hubert Van Zeller, O.S.B., *The Holy Rule*, New York: Sheed and Ward, 1958, p. 416.

5. Casey, p. 73.

6. For more information on *lectio divina*, consult Michael Casey, *Sacred Reading: The Ancient Art of Lectio Divina*, Liguori, MO: Triumph Books, 1996.

7. Anthony Mottola, Ph.D., trans., *The Spiritual Exercises of St. Ignatius*, Garden City, NY: Image Books, 1964, p. 108.

8. From "The Praises of the Virtues" in Thomas of Celano's *Second Life of St. Francis,* in *St. Francis of Assisi: Writings and Early Biographies*, Chicago: Franciscan Herald Press, 1973, p. 134.

9. St. John Damascene, *De imag.* 1.27:PG in *Catechism of the Catholic Church*, p. 329.

10. You can order icons from St. Isaac of Syria Skete (1-800-81-ICONS) or The Printery House (1-800-322-2737).

11. M. Helen Weier, O.S.C., *Festal Icons of the Lord*, Collegeville, MN: Liturgical Press, 1977, p. 6.

12. Henri Nouwen, *Behold the Beauty of the Lord: Praying With Icons*, Notre Dame, IN: Ave Maria Press, 1987, p. 14. This is a good book to consult if you are just beginning to pray with icons. You might also take a look at Jim Forest, *Praying with Icons*, Maryknoll, NY: Orbis Books, 1997.

13. *Shema Shlomo.* I, Hanhagot, p. 1.

14. *Or Tzaddikim,* p. 16a, 4:5-8.

15. Yitzhak Buxbaum, *Jewish Spiritual Practices,* Northvale, NJ: Jason Aronson, Inc., 1990, pp. 79-81. This is an excellent resource for Jewish spiritual practices.

16. Thomas Spidlik, *Drinking from the Hidden Fountain: A Patristic Breviary,* Kalamazoo, MI: Cistercian Publications, 1994, p. 367.

17. Yitzhak Buxbaum, p. 635.

18. Ibid., p. 109.

19. Ibid., p. 110.

20. Kavanaugh and Rodriguez, p. 264.

21. Ibid., p. 133.

22. An excellent resource for prayers of blessing is *Catholic Household Blessings and Prayers,* Collegeville, MN: The Liturgical Press, 1988.

23. Boniface Ramsey, O.P., ed., *John Cassian: The Conferences,* New York: Paulist Press, 1997, p. 380.

24. Anthony F. Chiffolo, *At Prayer With the Saints,* Liguori, MO: Liguori, 1998, p. 179.

25. Dorothy White, trans., *Pope John XXIII: Journal of a Soul,* New York: The New American Library, 1965, p. 411.

26. Marion A. Habig, ed., *St. Francis of Assisi: Writings and Early Biographies,* Chicago: Franciscan Herald Press, 1972, p. 465.